All About Roofs & Sidings

Created and Designed by the Editorial Staff of Ortho Books

Project Editor
Cheryl Smith

Writers
Kalton C. Lahue
T. Jeff Williams

Illustrators
Ron Hildebrand
Rik Olson

D0521759

Ortho Books

Publisher
Edward A. Evans

Editorial Director
Christine Jordan

Production Director
Ernie S. Tasaki

Managing Editors
Robert J. Beckstrom
Michael D. Smith
Sally W. Smith

System Manager
Linda M. Bouchard

Product Manager
Richard E. Pile, Jr.

Marketing Administrative Assistant
Daniel Stage

Distribution Specialist
Barbara F. Steadham

Operations Assistant
Georgiann Wright

Technical Consultant
J. A. Crozier, Jr., Ph.D.

Copy Chief
Melinda E. Levine

Editorial Coordinator
Cass Dempsey

Copyeditor
Barbara Feller-Roth

Proofreader
Elizabeth von Radics

Indexer
Shirley J. Manley

Editorial Assistants
Deborah Bruner
John Parr
Laurie A. Steele

Composition by
Nancy Patton Wilson-McCune

Production by
Studio 165

Separations by
Color Tech Corp.

Lithographed in the USA by
Webcrafters, Inc.

Additional Illustrator
Edith Allgood

Photographers
Names of photographers are followed by the page numbers on which their work appears.
R = right, C = center,
L = left, T = top, B = bottom.

Alside: 70, back cover TR
American Wood Council: 4–5
Laurie Black: 61, 97
Celotex: 3T, 16–17
Saxon Holt: 56
Saïd Nuseibeh: front cover, 1, 14, 26, 50, 90, back cover TL
John Parr: 89
Deborah Porter: 100
Shakertown: 3B, 64, back over BR
Stucco Stone: 99
Vinyl Siding Institute: 22, 69, 106, back cover BL

Special Thanks to
William Freistat
Chet Lindsey
Gary McCormick
Douglas A. Powell

Manufacturers and Suppliers
Alside; Akron, Ohio
The Breckenridge Company; Stockton, Calif.
Cedar Shake & Shingle Bureau; Bellevue, Wash.
Celotex; Tampa, Fla.
Del Monte Developers; Sunnyvale, Calif.
Piscatelli Custom Roofs; Berkeley, Calif.
Presley of Northern California; Walnut Creek, Calif.
Schaal Contracting; Hancock, N.H.
Shakertown; Winlock, Wash.
State Shingle Company; Oakland, Calif.
Douglas Stott; Berkeley, Calif.
Stucco Stone Products; Napa, Calif.
Vinyl Siding Institute; New York, N.Y.

Front Cover
The architectural planes and shapes of this home are emphasized by the crisp, simple lines of the siding and roofing materials. The traditional lap siding, plain board trim, and composition shingle roofing are all materials that can be applied by most homeowners with basic carpentry skills.

Title Page
Teamwork and automation facilitate the process of loading materials onto this rooftop.

Contents Page
Top: Composition shingles do not have to be boring.
Bottom: This contemporary home features shingle, panel, and curved panel sidings.

Back Cover
Top left: Getting materials up on the roof is one of the biggest challenges of roofing any home. This supplier has a truck with a conveyor belt to simplify the process.
Top right: Even new homes are being finished with vinyl siding.
Bottom left: Vinyl siding has renewed this home and made it nearly maintenance free.
Bottom right: The use of shingles and horizontal board siding adds handsome design elements to this home.

Address all inquiries to:
Ortho Books
Chevron Chemical Company
Consumer Products Division
Box 5047
San Ramon, CA 94583-0947

Copyright © 1984, 1991
Chevron Chemical Company
All rights reserved under international and Pan-American copyright conventions.

4 5 6 7 8 9
93 94 95 96

ISBN 0-89721-237-1
Library of Congress Catalog Card Number 90-86165

Chevron Chemical Company
6001 Bollinger Canyon Road, San Ramon, CA 94583

All About Roofs & Sidings

ROOFING & SIDING BASICS

Your home is probably your most important investment. Maintaining its value requires periodic attention to the protective exterior formed by the roof and siding, which are your home's first line of defense against the elements.

The roof and siding also constitute most of the decorative elements of your home's exterior. They should be appropriate to the style of the house, they should harmonize with one another, and they should be in good repair.

Whether you're remodeling or building, this book will provide the information you need to install and maintain roofing and siding, from start to finish. With the help of this book, you can make your roof and siding protect your home effectively and contribute to its good looks as well.

This first chapter introduces the subject and provides guidelines for inspecting and evaluating your present roof and siding. It will help you plan a new installation, accurately estimate time and costs involved, remind you about codes and permits, and help you decide if you need the services of a contractor. This chapter also introduces you to safety precautions that you should follow.

Light wood tones and white stucco combine to make this house fairly gleam. The steep roofs are balanced by the horizontal siding, and the soaring stucco chimneys tie it all together.

ROOF AND SIDING TERMS

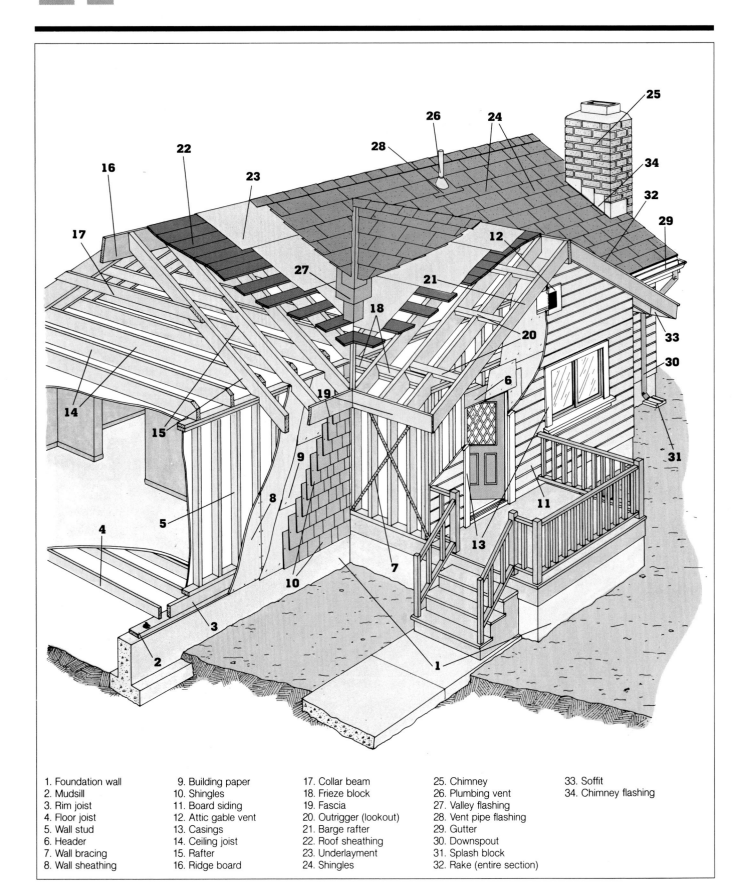

1. Foundation wall	9. Building paper	17. Collar beam	25. Chimney	33. Soffit
2. Mudsill	10. Shingles	18. Frieze block	26. Plumbing vent	34. Chimney flashing
3. Rim joist	11. Board siding	19. Fascia	27. Valley flashing	
4. Floor joist	12. Attic gable vent	20. Outrigger (lookout)	28. Vent pipe flashing	
5. Wall stud	13. Casings	21. Barge rafter	29. Gutter	
6. Header	14. Ceiling joist	22. Roof sheathing	30. Downspout	
7. Wall bracing	15. Rafter	23. Underlayment	31. Splash block	
8. Wall sheathing	16. Ridge board	24. Shingles	32. Rake (entire section)	

THE WELL-SEALED HOME

In a properly constructed building, weather protection begins at the ridge of the house—where the ridge shingles overlap the roof shingles—and ends where the bottom edge of the siding overlaps the foundation wall. In the area between the ridge and the foundation, each item of roof and siding overlaps the one below it, so that flowing water cannot find its way into the house.

The illustration below shows how the various elements of roofing and siding provide a protective skin. Even those items that don't show, such as the underlayment beneath the shingles and the building paper under the siding, must overlap.

The correct application of roofing and siding requires careful attention to detail. In new construction, the work proceeds from the inside out, with each succeeding layer protecting the one beneath it. From the illustration you can see, for instance, that a drip cap over a window is installed before the overlapping siding goes on, and the frieze blocks between rafters are placed to overlap the siding before the roof goes on. In doing a remodeling job, you must be careful to install or restore each piece in such a way as to maintain the protection originally built into the house.

Before you begin any work, whether it be new construction, remodeling, or repairs, be sure to read and understand the general section on roofing and siding and the section applying to the specific job you are tackling. Once you begin most jobs involving roofs and sidings, your house is open to the elements. A delay while you read further about what to do next could be costly if a storm should arrive.

This book will guide you in installing the roof and siding so that your house is properly protected. For information on other aspects of building and remodeling, consult Ortho's books *How to Replace & Install Doors & Windows, Basic Carpentry Techniques,* and *Basic Remodeling Techniques.*

The Protected Home

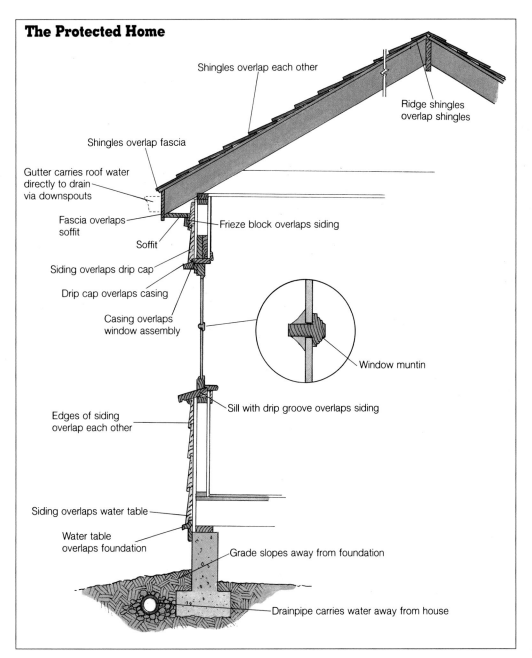

Shingles overlap each other

Ridge shingles overlap shingles

Shingles overlap fascia

Gutter carries roof water directly to drain via downspouts

Frieze block overlaps siding

Fascia overlaps soffit

Soffit

Siding overlaps drip cap

Drip cap overlaps casing

Casing overlaps window assembly

Window muntin

Sill with drip groove overlaps siding

Edges of siding overlap each other

Siding overlaps water table

Water table overlaps foundation

Grade slopes away from foundation

Drainpipe carries water away from house

If your roofing and siding concerns involve maintenance or remodeling of your house—as opposed to new construction—start by making a careful survey of the exterior of your house from top to bottom.

Looking for Roof Problems

First, stand back and look at your roof. If your house has composition shingles, as do the majority of houses in this country, look for dark patches, which indicate that the protective granules have worn away. These are weak spots in the roof. Look for badly cupped or curled shingles, caused by wind and temperature extremes. Water can work under the raised edges. On wood shake or shingle roofs, look for missing shingles. Once one is gone, the wind will start to pull others away.

Go up on the roof (see Safety Guidelines, pages 10 to 12) and look at the flashing around vent pipes, chimneys, and wall junctions. Cracks or gaps in caulking material are a possible leak source. Make sure that the flashing on the chimney is still firmly embedded in the mortar between the bricks. Loose mortar allows water to get behind the flashing.

Carefully check the valleys on the roof—these can be a source of trouble. Make sure that the valley material is undamaged and in good condition. In addition, make sure that the valleys are free of debris. Leaves and pine needles can dam up water and cause

it to run out the sides of the valley and under the shingles.

On flat roofs a low spot where water collects is potential trouble. Look for bubbles in a tar and gravel roof, which often indicate that moisture has worked its way beneath the underlayment. Fix any bubbles (see page 104).

Position a ladder against the side of the house and check the eaves of the roof. This is a particularly common area for rot to set in, because water can be driven up under the shingles by rain or freezing action. Push the tip of a screwdriver into the wood on the edge of the eaves. Any place where the screwdriver penetrates much beyond ¼ inch probably has wood rot. Fortunately, any rot in these areas generally does not extend far up the roof and can be repaired without much difficulty when a new roof is applied. Take a good look at the gutters while you are up there. They should be clean, without sags, and firmly in place.

Now take a good flashlight and go into the attic. Carefully inspect each rafter. Even if you haven't seen a leak in the house, water could be leaking through the roof, running down a rafter, and dropping between the siding and the inside wall, a situation you can spot by telltale water stains on the rafter. Use your screwdriver to poke any suspicious-looking spots for possible rot.

Looking for Siding Problems

Take a careful look at the siding. It may have problems, but generally there will be fewer than you might find on a roof, because it is less subject to sun and storm damage.

Look at the paint job first. If you see extensive bubbling, cracking, or peeling, it may mean that you have insufficient vapor-barrier protection in the house. This can happen if your house is not insulated, or if the insulation does not have a vapor barrier on it, such as the aluminum foil on insulation batts. A vapor barrier is designed to stop the moisture generated inside your house— by such activities as breathing, washing dishes, doing laundry, and bathing—from moving through the walls, where it may condense on meeting cold outside air. The vapor can move through the house sheathing and literally push the paint off it. One solution, short of tearing off the inside walls and installing vapor barriers, is to add vents inside the house and install dehumidifiers.

Look for any cracks in the exterior sheathing. Water can work its way through a crack to the inside of the wall and cause wood rot.

Check the trim around the doors and windows and at the corners of the building. It should be firmly in place and well caulked. There should be a tight seal where the siding meets any chimney masonry.

How to Find A Leak

Leaks in the roof may be difficult to find. Rarely, for instance, does a leak in the ceiling come from a spot directly above in the roof. Instead, it may have traveled a considerable distance along the roof deck or a rafter before appearing.

When a leak does develop, go outside and see if you can spot a loose or missing shingle. If there is nothing obviously wrong on the roof, go into the attic. Darken the attic and look for a ray of light, which indicates a hole. Search carefully around vent pipes, chimneys, skylights, and valley flashing. With the exception of valley flashing, these are areas where the roof deck has been cut through and then sealed. The seal, or flashing material, is often the culprit. In the case of valley flashing, the leak is generally caused by an obstruction in the valley that causes water to pool behind it, or by poor workmanship. Mark any holes you find by driving nails through them or inserting a piece of wire, such as a straightened coat hanger, to help you relocate the holes from the roof.

Starting from above the leak in the ceiling, look for water running down a rafter. Follow that up the rafter. If it disappears, it is most likely running along the side or top of the rafter. You may have to pull away insulation to trace the water. If the insulation is wet, remove that section by cutting above and below the damp area with a knife. Dry the damp insulation, then staple it back up after the leak is fixed. Wet insulation is an invitation to mildew and rot. If the attic has been insulated with fiberglass blankets, wear protective clothing, including gloves, safety glasses or goggles, and a protective mask, during your inspection.

Do not go up on a roof in a rainstorm. Just put out a pan to catch the drip and wait until the roof is dry. When you do get on the roof to pinpoint the leak, use a hose to flood the suspected area with water while someone in the attic watches for the drip. Begin watering the area below where you think the leak might be and slowly work your way up.

Planning a New Roof or Siding

There are a number of factors to take into consideration when planning to install a new roof or siding, among them choosing an appropriate system, estimating the cost, and estimating how much time the project will take.

What Style?

Installation of a new roof or siding provides an opportunity to change the way your house looks. If your house has a particular style, you'll probably want to keep that look, or perhaps even carry it further—replacing composition shingles with shakes, for instance, to complement a Colonial. Or you may want to modernize an old-fashioned house. Whatever your preference, be sure to read through the rest of this book before making your decision. The slope of your roof may limit your choices; the application of some materials—such as a slate roof—is beyond the scope of the do-it-yourselfer, and thus of this book, because the work requires professional skills.

Once you know the practical limitations on the choice of style, give yourself some time to consider the variety of options remaining. The photographs throughout this book can help you focus on the possibilities. Lumberyards and roofing centers can show you some ideas, and manufacturers are happy to mail brochures that show what their products can do. You might consider, for instance, adding antique molding to the trim on your home, or putting fancy-cut shingle siding on dormers.

If you plan on radically altering your house's appearance, consider how it will fit into the neighborhood when you are finished. Ordinarily, a new roof or new siding won't raise any eyebrows, but a radical departure from the norm—say, a shimmering aluminum panel roof in a line of houses covered with sedate dark shingles—may make you an unwelcome neighbor.

How Much Will It Cost?

New roofing and siding projects are expensive, but sooner or later must be done. Many roofs don't last much beyond 25 years. Siding, depending on the quality of material and paint, may hold up longer, but it won't last forever.

While these jobs may be expensive, they will cost you only half as much if you do the work yourself. It takes some skill and hard work, but you can do it—and do it right—with a little patience.

How Much Time Will It Take?

Fair warning is needed here: Never underestimate the time needed for roofing and siding projects. Sit down and make some careful estimates, using the instructions in this book as a guide to the magnitude of the job. Whatever time you come up with, double it—and even then have contingency plans for unexpected delays.

For openers, it's a roofer's law that no matter what time of the year you take off the old roof, you can expect it to rain. Even if it hasn't rained for three months, count on showers when the old roof is removed. You can protect your house (see page 26), but you won't be able to work until the rain stops.

More possible delays: You find rotted roof-deck boards under the old roof that must be replaced; a rafter has to be fixed; you find that you need to replace the gutters too; or the flashing around the chimney is worn out and must be replaced.

Putting on new siding is not as subject to unexpected delays—the eaves will provide considerable protection in inclement weather, for instance—but it too can be a time-consuming job.

This list of potential calamities is not meant to discourage you, only to make you aware of the possibilities. A job with no adverse surprises is a pleasure, and a rare one at that.

Codes and Permits

Virtually every house built or remodeled in this country must adhere to one of the national model building codes, or a local one. Such codes are designed to ensure safe construction practices. When you undertake any construction project, you usually must have a permit issued by your local building inspector, but installing a new roof or siding on an existing house may not require one. To find out, you will have to call your inspection department and inquire. In roofing, the concern is whether the new roof will add too much weight to the rafters. For siding, there will be such questions as whether, when you remove the old siding and put on the new, the walls will still be structurally braced. Local codes vary so widely that you will have to discuss your situation with the building inspection department. The permits are not particularly expensive, so don't try to do without one—this could get you fined.

SAFETY GUIDELINES

Working on a steep roof or standing on a high ladder to do a siding job has one obvious risk—it's a long way to the ground. Working without proper precautions or being careless on the job is an invitation to trouble. But by staying alert and using proper safety equipment and techniques, you can make your job trouble free.

The Worker

If you are nervous about being on a roof or high on a ladder, don't force yourself to do it. Many people are disconcerted by heights. Telling yourself that you are going to do it anyway may be courting disaster. Work your way up slowly—over a few days, perhaps—to see if you become accustomed to the height. If you still feel afraid, hire a qualified person to do the job.

If the work starts going badly and your frustration rises, take a break. Getting angry and hurrying the job only invites more mistakes. The job should be relatively pleasant. After all, you're doing it on your own time.

On a roof or a ladder, wear soft-soled shoes, such as tennis shoes, to minimize the chances of slipping. Shirt and pants should be loose and nonbinding so that you can move about easily. Wear a hat to protect your head from the sun. Roofing and siding jobs can be long ones, so stay comfortable.

Wear protective eye gear when chipping concrete or when using a power saw to cut metal, fiberglass, or masonry.

Rules of the Roof

Knowing and following a few simple rules will help you to complete the job safely.

• Wear rubber-soled shoes, as noted above, to minimize the chances of slipping or damaging the roof. Make sure that the soles are clean and dry.
• Always wear gloves when working with metal, to avoid cuts from sharp edges.
• Never go up on the roof when it is raining, when the roof is wet, or if a lightning storm is imminent. Work only when the weather is dry and warm, with no strong winds blowing.
• Keep the roof clear of debris. Stepping on a scrap of underlayment can send you flying in a split second. Watch out for loose shingles or tiles, moss, and wet leaves.
• When removing an old roof, work from the top down and keep the roof clean by sweeping periodically. Debris should be dumped in a container directly from the roof, if possible. When throwing things from the roof edge, be careful not to overbalance.
• Rope off the area where you are dumping debris so that no one strays into this free-fire zone. Be especially careful to keep pets and small children away from your work area to avoid possible injury caused by falling materials.
• Keep your distance from power lines attached to the roof and avoid energized television and FM antennas.
• When stacking materials on the roof, disperse them evenly to spread the load. If the roof is too steep to keep shingle bundles from sliding, nail roofing jacks near the ridge and install planks to assist in keeping the bundles in place.
• If your roof has a slope of 5 in 12 or less (see page 19 for calculating roof slope), working comfortably should not be a problem. But on roofs with a steeper slope, you may need to take some extra precautions. Working next to the eaves when applying the first few courses on a steep roof is awkward and dangerous. Use ladders and a scaffold plank if possible when applying the first courses, to provide enough room for you to sit on the roof as you shingle.
• If it is not possible to use scaffolding, tie yourself to a rope that goes over the ridge and is well secured on the other side to a tree, porch upright, or the like.
• Use ladder jacks or a roofer's seat as described on pages 12 and 52 as you continue up steeply sloped roofs.
• Don't strain or overexert yourself. Lift only what is comfortable for you; it's better to split the load than to strain your back.
• Set a steady pace that's comfortable, then maintain it, taking frequent breaks to prevent fatigue from setting in. When it does, quit work. In this way you will stay alert and not take any chances.

• Make sure that you are well balanced and on solid footing when using a pneumatic hammer or stapler. These tools are very powerful and can cause severe injury to your hand or foot if improperly positioned when triggered. Make sure that the air hose does not get tangled around your feet or hung up on some part of the roof.

Ladders, Scaffolding, And Roofing Jacks

A variety of devices is available to raise you to the height needed to work on the roof. Each requires caution and respect at all times to avoid a mishap.

Ladders

The extension ladder is the basic tool for all roofing and siding work. It allows you to climb to working heights, and to carry materials from the ground to where they are needed. Extension ladders are manufactured of wood, aluminum, or fiberglass. All are equally good.

Wood ladders are solid and heavy, and offer a high degree of psychological assurance for those who might be a bit squeamish about climbing off the ground. Many people simply feel safer climbing or standing on a wood ladder.

Aluminum ladders are lightweight and most can be handled easily by one person, but they must be kept away from contact with power lines to avoid a serious shock. Fiberglass ladders possess qualities similar to those of aluminum ladders but eliminate the chance of shock from power lines.

Using a Ladder Safely

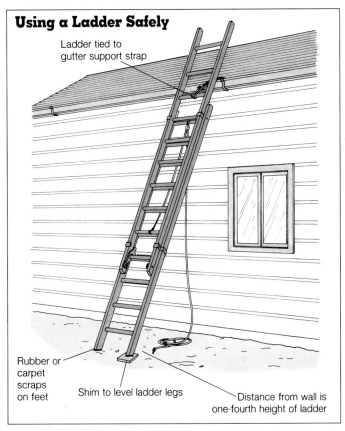

Ladder tied to gutter support strap

Rubber or carpet scraps on feet

Shim to level ladder legs

Distance from wall is one-fourth height of ladder

Pump Jack

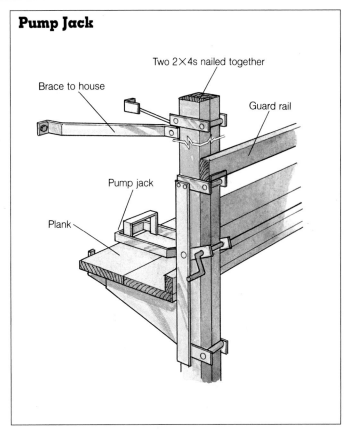

Two 2×4s nailed together

Brace to house

Guard rail

Pump jack

Plank

Correct use of ladders is of paramount importance. Many people start thinking about ladder safety only after a near mishap. Here are a few guidelines for proper ladder use.

• Before using a ladder, check that all the rungs are solid. See that there are no loose screws or rivets.

• Make sure that the pulleys and locking devices on extension ladders work smoothly and securely.

• Sight along a ladder to see that it is not warped or bent. This could cause it to collapse when weight is placed above the warped or bent area.

• Raise a long ladder by having a friend brace the bottom with his or her feet while you walk it up over your head from the other end.

• If a friend is not available, place the ladder base against the house and walk the ladder into an upright position, then carefully move the base of the ladder outward from the house.

• When you raise a metal ladder, make sure that it does not come in contact with overhead power lines.

• Once a ladder is positioned against the house, set the ladder base away from the house by a distance equal to one fourth of the working height of the ladder.

• Set the ladder feet on firm and level ground. If one leg must be shimmed to keep it level, use a single scrap of the right height. Don't build up a series of blocks.

• A ladder placed on a smooth concrete surface may slip. Prevent this by using rubber safety shoes on the ladder feet,

or by gluing rubber or indoor-outdoor carpeting to the bottom of the feet.

• Extend a ladder to its working height only after it has been positioned properly against the house. Never extend a ladder more than 80 to 85 percent of its rated height. A 15 to 20 percent overlap of the sections will make the upper section more stable when you are working on it.

• When possible, have someone steady a ladder while you are climbing. Only one person at a time should climb a ladder.

• Stay off a ladder during bad weather or high winds.

• When working with a long extension ladder, keep the ladder from slipping to the side by tying the top securely to a gutter support strap.

• When working on a ladder, don't lean out in an attempt to reach beyond arm's length. Keep your body inside the ladder rails.

• When working from a ladder placed on the roof, secure the ladder over the ridge of the roof with a metal ladder bracket or similar device.

Scaffolding

A ladder has severe limitations as a work platform. But scaffolding greatly speeds up a siding job by providing a work platform along which you can move without constantly moving ladders. Remember, however, that scaffolding is considered a leading cause of construction accidents by the Occupational Safety and Health Administration (OSHA). If you use scaffolding it must be properly constructed.

Ladder Jacks

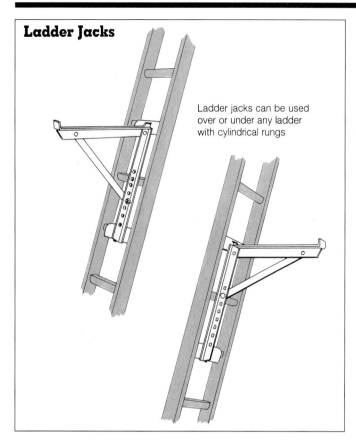

Ladder jacks can be used over or under any ladder with cylindrical rungs

Lumberyards offer a full 2-inch by 9-inch plank of scaffold-grade rough-sawn spruce. The rough surface prevents slipping and the greater thickness makes the platform more substantial than ordinary lumber. You can use a single plank, but placing two planks side by side to form an 18-inch platform is even better, because the wider area is safer and more easily accommodates your tools and materials. Cleat the two planks together with pieces of plywood nailed on the underside at 4-foot intervals.

A less expensive but equally efficient alternative is to make your own composite plank by nailing a 24-inch-wide strip of ¾-inch plywood to two good Douglas fir 2 by 4s placed on edge. A plank made this way is not only rigid but will easily support a load of several hundred pounds.

Regardless of the type of plank used, make sure that each end extends at least 6 inches beyond the support, since your weight will cause the plank to bend and pull the ends away from the supports. The standard length for a scaffold plank is 13 feet, giving a working span of about 12 feet after overlap. Twelve feet is the maximum length generally recommended for using a wood plank. If you need to span a longer distance, an extendable aluminum plank or platform can be rented. Whatever you do, don't put your weight on the overlap in an effort to get to a hard-to-reach area. This will cause the other end of the plank to raise up, which can lead to a serious accident.

You can create a scaffold with a pair of sawhorses or wood trestles. Stepladders are not suitable for use as scaffold supports. They are unstable and can accommodate only a single-plank width. For greater heights, you might want to rent ladder jacks, which fit over the ladder rungs (see illustration at left).

Pipe scaffolding can be rented from lumberyards and equipment supply companies. This tubular, welded-frame scaffolding is versatile and safe, provides ample working space, and can be erected or dismantled by one person. If you can complete the job quickly, the rental cost may be within your budget, since this type of scaffolding will let you work even faster than plank scaffolding. However, the cost of rental can prove exorbitant if your project is done over an extended period of time, such as at night and on weekends.

Pump jacks are movable steel brackets that can be used to construct a more versatile scaffold that can be moved up and down easily. This type of scaffold lets you adjust the plank or platform to a convenient working height by operating the jacks with your foot. Since the uprights must be set in shallow holes and anchored to the house wall with steel braces, it may take you some time to set up, dismantle, and move the scaffolding as you work your way around the house to apply siding.

Pump jack components also can be rented, but make sure that the set you get is clean and free from rust, and shows no signs of deterioration. Pay particular attention to the condition of the cotter pins used to hold the components together.

Roofing Jacks

Sometimes called roof brackets or toe board jacks, roofing jacks are lengths of metal strap that hold a board, which helps support you and your materials on a steep roof (see page 28 for illustration). Most of your weight stays on the roof, but the board keeps you in place. You also can walk back and forth on the roof with part of your weight on the board. Roofing jacks can be used on all types of roofing.

One end of the roofing jack has notches so that it can be nailed to the roof; the other end has an angle to hold the edge of a board. Roofing jacks come in different sizes and shapes; the one that holds a 2 by 4 on edge is excellent. To avoid the risk of having the board break under your weight, do not use a board longer than 10 feet unless you use a third bracket in the center for support.

Roofing jacks should always be nailed firmly through the decking and into a rafter, using 16-penny (16d) common nails, not ordinary roofing nails. Always put the nails where they will be covered by a subsequent course of shingles.

If you have never seen roofing jacks in use, you may wonder how it is possible to nail a jack to the roof, cover it with several courses of shingles, then remove it and move up. The answer is in the shape of the top of the jack. When you want to remove the jack, tap the bottom with the hammer until it slides up free of the nails, pull to one side, and slide it out. Then gently lift up the shingle tab and pound the exposed nail head flush to the roof deck.

WHO WILL DO THE WORK

You can install many kinds of siding or make minor repairs to your roofing by following the directions in this book. However, when it comes to installing a new roof, you need to take into consideration many more factors.

The lure of saving a sizable part of the cost by doing the work yourself makes it easy to overlook some important factors. One of the first questions to ask yourself is how fast you can do the work.

If you are removing an old roof, or if you are working on new construction, you must get the roof on quickly. Don't even imagine what your house would look like after a thundershower put 2 inches of rain in the attic.

Consider your willingness and ability to do the physical labor involved in roofing. Heavy materials have to be toted around, often to substantial heights. It's hard, repetitious, and sometimes hazardous work that can be hot and extremely tiring. You'll be spending many hours hammering. Be sure that you are both mentally and physically able to undertake the work; otherwise, you may find yourself calling in a professional to finish your half-done job.

If you plan to work on the project while you pursue your regular profession, and do all of the construction in the evenings and on weekends, it will take you much longer than it would if you hired professionals. Inspectors and some suppliers are available only during regular business hours, and someone will have to be home during the week to work with them.

In estimating job time, you should allow two hours to put down the first square (100 square feet) of shingles. The second square will go a little faster, and by the second day you might be putting down one square per hour. By comparison, a professional can lay two squares or more an hour.

The slope of your roof also will be a consideration in your decision to do the work yourself or hire a contractor. If the roof is very steep or is two or more stories high and has numerous dormers or a turret or two, you had better get a contractor. But if you have a more standard roof, you can probably do it yourself.

Certain roofs—tar and gravel, slate or tile, and aluminum shingles, for instance—should be done professionally. If one of these is your choice, or if you're hesitant about installing one of the other roofs yourself, you should call in a contractor.

How to Hire A Contractor

You can hire a contractor to do your entire roof or to help with some parts of the job. Finding the right contractor, however, is as important as selecting materials and estimating costs.

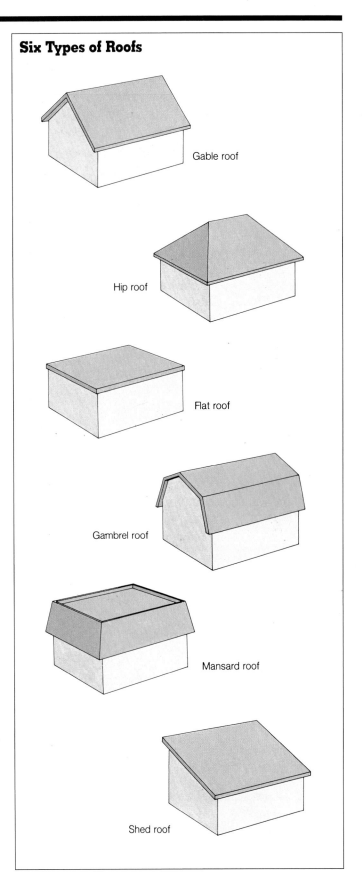

Six Types of Roofs

Gable roof

Hip roof

Flat roof

Gambrel roof

Mansard roof

Shed roof

If possible, select a contractor whose work you know, or one who has done a similar job for a friend or neighbor. Otherwise, check under Roofing Contractors in the Yellow Pages of your telephone directory, or contact trade associations or local suppliers for recommendations.

Contractors are licensed by most states. They must include their license number on any contract, and you can go to the state contractors' licensing board with any complaint you might have.

Get the names of several professionals and ask them to bid on your job. Going with the lowest bid does not guarantee that you will be satisfied with the quality of the service. Distinguish clearly between your role and that of the contractor, and set definite terms for change orders to handle any contingencies. A change order is a written agreement between

These lightweight concrete tiles are a durable, maintenance-free roofing material that gives the home a feeling of permanence and elegance. These tiles are installed by hooking them over 1 by 2 wood strips. The strips are nailed to the solid plywood sheathing after an underlayment of roofing paper has been applied. Notice the special tiles for covering the ridges, hips, and rakes.

the owner and the contractor directing adjustments or additions to the original plans once construction has begun. Contingencies are the surprises that crop up along the way. All this will help to reduce the number of variables and make a fixed-bid contract go more smoothly.

You also may consider negotiating a time-and-materials contract whereby the contractor bills you for time on a per-hour basis and for the materials purchased for your job. The advantages of such a contract are that you pay only the actual cost of the job, and you usually get more attentive service than with a fixed bid. The disadvantages are that you don't know exactly how much the job will cost until it is finished, and you don't know what it would have cost to have another contractor do the same job. The main thing to recognize is that you are shopping for a service, not a product such as an automobile.

If you solicit fixed bids, the following guidelines will help you observe the correct bidding etiquette.

• Do not initiate a formal bid process if you already have a contractor in mind. Just negotiate directly.

• Briefly describe the project in your initial phone call to each prospective contractor.

• Have ready a list of questions: how long the contractor has been in business, experience with similar jobs, method of scheduling the work, and references.

• Check references by following up on the contractor's personal recommendations. Visit job sites and completed projects. Ask previous clients if they were satisfied with the contractor's performance and attitude.

• Contact the local Better Business Bureau to determine if complaints have been filed against the contractor. If so, check with local authorities about any pending lawsuits.

• After narrowing your choices to three or four people, set a firm date for receiving bids.

• Specify what, if any, materials and labor you yourself intend to provide.

• If a bidder requests clarification or information, answer the request in writing. Send a copy of your answer, labeled Addendum, to each bidder.

• Use the same process to notify bidders of any changes that occur in your plans.

• Along with the price quote, request a copy of the contract form that the bidder expects you to sign, as well as the bidder's credit references.

• Review the bids and forms. In some cases a bid doubles as a contract. For this reason it should contain what the contractor will do and what materials will be used, the time frame in which the work will be done, the payment schedule, and the guarantee.

The selection of a contractor should be based on several factors: personal rapport, experience with similar jobs, references and recommendations, schedules (yours and the contractor's), and cost. The low bid is not necessarily the one to choose. It may indicate the potential for sloppy work, inadequate supervision, or serious oversights. It also may lead to costly changes later on. It is unethical to negotiate simultaneously with two contractors after you have received their bids, or to invite another contractor to compete after the bidding process has closed. Remember to notify all parties of your choice and of the winning bid price, and thank them for taking the time to bid.

Always insist on a well-written and complete contract. It does not have to be elaborate; since most contractors already have their own contract form, you can use that as a starting point. Not all of the following provisions will apply to your particular situation, but a good contract should include most of these points.

• Stipulation that all permits are to be obtained by the contractor and all work done according to the local code.

• Specified start and completion dates, with a detailed schedule, as well as how the contractor will compensate you if the job is not completed on time.

• Clear delineation of the contractor's duties and of your own, including all preparation and cleanup steps.

• A list of all materials that you will be supplying, and all materials that the contractor will use in the job. Such lists should include brand names and weights or grades of the materials to avoid any misunderstanding.

• A payment schedule in which the contractor agrees that you pay no more than one quarter of the fee in advance, with other increments to follow at specified periods.

• A provision for the contractor to supply lien releases from all subcontractors and suppliers before final payment is made.

• Requirements for final payment, including final inspection by the building inspection department (if applicable). Maintain a 30-day waiting period prior to payment to ensure that you are satisfied with the work that has been done.

• A written guarantee of the work to be done and the specified time period the guarantee will cover.

• A written statement that the contractor carries worker's compensation insurance.

• A specific procedure for handling change orders.

• Specified procedures for communication when more than one professional is involved.

• A method for resolving potential disputes.

You may wish to try a specialist rather than a contractor. A specialist is essentially a skilled worker who is not licensed; any dispute with a specialist would have to be worked out with that individual alone. Many specialists do work that is just as good as a contractor's; they also may work for less. However, with a specialist, you may have to pay a worker's compensation insurance fee to protect yourself in the event of an on-the-job injury. Check with your own insurance agent on this matter. You may also be liable for employment taxes. It is advisable to seek the advice of a tax accountant before hiring anyone.

ROOFS

Regardless of the material used, your roof will eventually need repair or replacement. A roof that leaks should be corrected before it leads to more costly structural problems.

This chapter will give you the information needed to select the right roof and plan its installation. There's a complete section devoted to composition shingles, the most popular and the easiest for the do-it-yourselfer to install. In addition, you'll find a full explanation of installing shakes, wood shingles, tile, roll roofing, and panel roofing, as well as complete instructions for installing flashing, gutters, and downspouts.

The first duty of a roof is to protect, but it should also be attractive and blend with the style and color of the house.

CHOOSING THE RIGHT ROOF

If you are building a new home or doing extensive structural remodeling, you can choose the style of the roof. Otherwise, you can choose among the materials available for roofing but they must be suited to the structure of your existing house.

Roof Styles

None of the six basic roof styles illustrated on page 13 is particularly better than another, but some are better suited to certain parts of the country. Flat roofs are common in much of the Southwest, for example, where there is relatively little rain or snow. However, such a roof would not be practical in states that often endure heavy snowfalls, or even in high elevations in the Southwest. There you commonly find steep gable or hip roofs that readily shed snow.

Roof style dictates roofing material to some degree. Flat roofs, for example, are almost always covered with tar and gravel, making what is called a built-up roof. Polyurethane foam can be sprayed on either an existing roof or new roof decking to form a lightweight and durable roof that also insulates. A flat roof with a deck built over it might call for one of the elastomeric roofing membranes, applied in either liquid or solid sheets and built up in several coats. Cold mop roofing, using a liquid with an asphalt base, is used mostly for small repairs only.

A nearly flat roof might also be covered with asphalt roll roofing, which is inexpensive but unlikely to last beyond 10 years. Built-up roofs are widely used on roofs with up to a 3 in 12 slope (see page 19 for calculating roof slope), but not greater than that, because the hot tar runs off when it is applied.

With some special preparation, composition shingles can be put on roofs with as little as a 2 in 12 slope. However, a steeper (4 in 12) slope is greatly preferred in order to shed water more quickly. Shake and shingle roofs should also have at least a 4 in 12 slope to shed rainwater efficiently.

Issues to Consider In Choosing A Material

There are many issues to consider when choosing a roofing material. The slope of your roof may eliminate some choices. The existing material may rule out others if you're applying the new roof over an old one. You should certainly be pleased with how the material looks, but also consider its durability and resistance to fire.

Slope of the Roof

The slope, or pitch, of your roof is important in deciding what type of roofing material can be used, and whether a homeowner can work safely on the roof or should consider hiring a professional.

Most do-it-yourselfers can work safely on their roof as long as the slope is no steeper than 6 in 12.

Covering Old Roofing

The easiest way to a new roof is to apply it directly over the existing surface. This approach generally requires a minimum of preparation, saving the time and expense of stripping off the old roof. You will, however, have to remove material from the ridge and install new flashing. In addition, using the old roof as the deck for the new one gives an extra layer of insulation. Under certain conditions, however, you will have to remove the old roof before installing a new one.

If the old roof is in such bad shape that it does not present a uniform base to which the new one can be nailed, it is better to strip it down to the sheathing. In such cases, you often will find that water has rotted the sheathing, which will require repair before the new roof can be installed.

Local building codes also determine the maximum number of reroofs allowed on the framework. The general rule of thumb for wood shingle roofs is the original and one reroof; for other types of roofs, you may be allowed the original and two reroofs. Be sure to check this with your local building inspection department.

Old tile and slate roofs must be completely removed when reroofing. Shake roofs, which do not offer the smooth, flat surface required for installation of a new roof, must also be removed.

If you plan on leaving the old roof in place, the type of material used for a new roof will depend on the old surface. You can roof over composition shingles with more composition shingles, wood shingles, or shakes. If the old roof is wood shingles, you can reroof with wood or asphalt.

Tile can be installed over composition or wood shingle roofs, but its much greater weight introduces the factor of whether the house framing and rafters can structurally support it. If your roof is now covered with composition or wood shingles, but you want clay tiles or slate, it is unlikely that the rafters can support the load. You could switch to the lighter concrete tiles, or the problem might be remedied with a support system in the attic. A contractor can advise you on this. It may be necessary to remove the old roof in order to lighten the load.

Another consideration is the slope of your roof. The lower the slope, the slower the roof sheds water. A roof that doesn't shed water rapidly requires more precautions to avoid leaks. A roof that is completely flat should be covered by soldered metal or built-up roofing. Metal panels can be put on slopes as low as 2 in 12; on low-slope roofs they should overlay by at least 18 inches to prevent leaks. Use roll roofing on slopes of 1 in 12 or 2 in 12. See pages 62 to 63 for application instructions for roll roofing.

As the slope of a roof increases, so does the range of practical materials. Composition shingles are commonly used on roofs with slopes of 4 in 12 or more. On roofs with slopes of less than 4 in 12,

Two Methods of Determining Roof Slope

The slope, or pitch, of your roof is important in deciding what type of roofing material you can put on it. There are two basic ways to determine roof slope.

If you can readily get on your roof, you can easily calculate the slope with a straight board, a bubble level, and a ruler. Place the board, which need be only about 3 feet long, on the roof. Check that it closely conforms to the slope of the roof and is not pushed out of line by a rock or a warped shingle. Measure and mark off 12 inches on the level. Place one end of the level near the top of the board and raise the other end of the level until the bubbles are centered. Holding the ruler so that it is straight up and down, measure the distance from the top of the board to the bottom of the level at the 12-inch mark. The ratio of that distance to 12 inches tells you the roof slope. If the distance is 6 inches, it means that the roof rises 6 inches for every 12 inches of horizontal run. Slopes normally range from 1 in 12 (nearly flat) to 12 in 12 (45-degree angle typical of an A-frame) and normally do not come in half-inch increments.

Another way to check the roof slope is with a tool called a Squangle®. This adjustable device, available in most hardware stores, is used in laying out and cutting rafters. Just place it against an exposed rafter end or a block placed against the fascia board, adjust until it lines up with the angle of the roof, and read the scale.

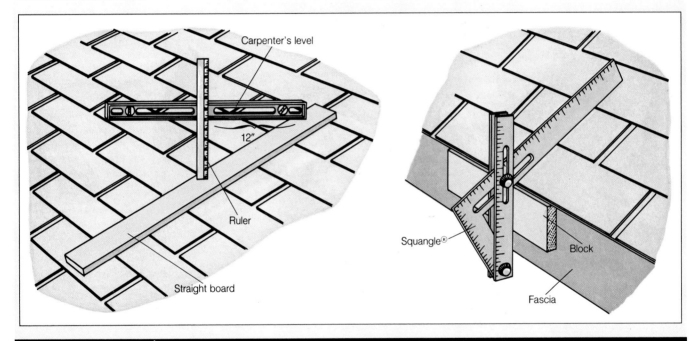

Carpenter's level

12"

Ruler

Straight board

Squangle®

Block

Fascia

wind can force rain under composition shingles, or tear them away altogether. You'll also need to take special precautions when applying composition shingles on very steep slopes, more than 21 in 12, as detailed on page 50.

Shakes, wood shingles, and tile should not be put on slopes of less than 4 in 12, since the lower slopes make them too vulnerable to wind-driven rain.

Aesthetics

The new roof you choose should harmonize with the type of siding presently on the house. However, if you also plan on installing new siding, select the roof to match the new siding. Check around your neighborhood and you'll see that the use of two or three exterior colors generally offers the greatest visual appeal. Earth tones and weathered colors work best with natural settings and let the roof blend in, whereas bright colors stand out and emphasize the roof over the rest of the structure. Dark colors make the house appear lower; light colors have the opposite effect. Consult the chart on page 23 for guidance on colors.

Durability

This is a rough guide to the length of time a properly maintained roof will last in a temperate climate. Tile and slate roofs are the most durable, with an approximate minimum life of 50 years, followed by shakes and metal panels, with a minimum 25-year life. Composition and wood shingles can last a minimum of 12 to 15 years. Roll roofing and built-up roofing are the least durable, with an approximate minimum 10-year life.

Fire Resistance

All roofing materials are tested by Underwriter's Laboratories (UL, an independent testing service) and given a rating of A, B, or C, with A being the highest in fire resistance. The UL ratings are as follows.
• Class A: capable of withstanding severe exposure to fire
• Class B: capable of withstanding moderate exposure to fire
• Class C: capable of withstanding light exposure to fire

In order to qualify for a UL rating, the material being tested by flame must not blow off or fall off the roof as flaming brands, must not break or crack to expose the roof deck, and must not allow continued flaming on the underside of the roof deck.

Whatever type of roof you install, overhead tree limbs and other foliage should be trimmed back so that they do not present an additional hazard.

Composition Shingles

In composition shingles look for a Class A rating. Composition roofing manufacturers voluntarily send samples of their products to the independent UL to be tested. Roofing manufacturers that are granted a UL rating are proud of it and will prominently display it on each bundle of composition shingles. Don't use composition shingles that are not so marked.

Wood Shingles And Shakes

Unless treated with a retardant, shakes and wood shingles are quite susceptible to fire. The UL-approved, fire-retardant, pressure-treated shakes and wood shingles are more expensive but are safer in fire-risk areas. They may be required by local building codes. However, some cities recently have taken steps to ban wood shingle roofs on the basis that even treated wood is not sufficiently fire resistant to merit its continued use on new homes or as a replacement roof.

Slate, Tile, And Metal Panels

These materials are not just fire resistant but actually fireproof. However, metal has a low fire rating because it conducts heat so readily.

Tar and Gravel And Roll Roofing

Both materials are fire resistant. Prolonged exposure to fire, however, would eventually cause either to burn.

Cost

The better the material, the more expensive it will be, but the longer your roof will last. Slate, tile, shake, and wood shingle roofs are all beautiful and of high quality but they are expensive. However, you can reduce the price of a shake or wood shingle roof by applying it yourself, saving considerably on labor costs.

Roll roofing, metal panels, and tar and gravel are less expensive materials, but you give up something in appearance when you use them on a residence.

Between the two extremes are composition shingles—attractive, long lasting, and relatively inexpensive. These qualities, plus the fact that a do-it-yourselfer can apply them, have made composition shingles the most widely used roofing material in this country.

Types of Roofing Materials

The accompanying illustration will help to familiarize you with the various materials available for roofing. Be sure to read all about those materials you are considering for use.

Composition Shingles

It is estimated that more than 70 percent of the houses in this country are roofed with composition shingles. They are available in a wide array of colors, weights, textures, and edge configurations.

Composition shingles have a central core made from cellulose fibers or fiberglass that is coated with asphalt on both sides and topped with a protective mineral aggregate. These shingles have a Class A fire rating. (Felt core shingles, if you can still find them, are rated Class C, and are not desirable.)

Of all the different types of shingles available, the easiest for the do-it-yourselfer to apply—and the most widely sold—are three-tab composition shingles (see illustration, page 21). They are 12 inches wide and 36 inches long. (Increasingly, shingles are being made in metric measurements. Be sure that you know what you have purchased, and check the manufacturer's installation instructions. The instructions in this book use inches and feet. A metric conversion chart appears on page 112.) Three-tab shingles come in different qualities, judged primarily by their weight per square (the quantity needed to cover 100 square feet). The heavier the shingle, the longer it is guaranteed to last. Standard shingle weights run from 215 to 300 pounds per square and are designed to last 15 to 30 years. Composition shingles can also be two tab, one tab, or interlocking, but these variations are less available in stores nowadays.

Composition shingles are now commonly made with strips of roofing cement to seal the tab of the course applied above them. After the shingle is applied, the heat of the sun melts the strip and bonds the two shingles together.

Ideally, composition shingles should be laid when the temperature is between 40° and 85° F. In cold weather they should be stored in a warm area prior to installation.

Wood Shingles And Shakes

Shingles are smaller and lighter than shakes and commonly are sawn on both sides, which gives them their typical shape. Shakes are usually split by hand, which helps account for their higher cost. Both shingles and shakes are mostly cut from western red cedar.

Shakes and shingles are graded by number—1 (the best), 2, and 3. For roofs, use only 1. Cut from heartwood, it is highly resistant to rot and free of knots. Originally, grade 1 was cut only from first-growth timber and would last for 50 years or more. Now, with prime forests mostly

Roofing Materials

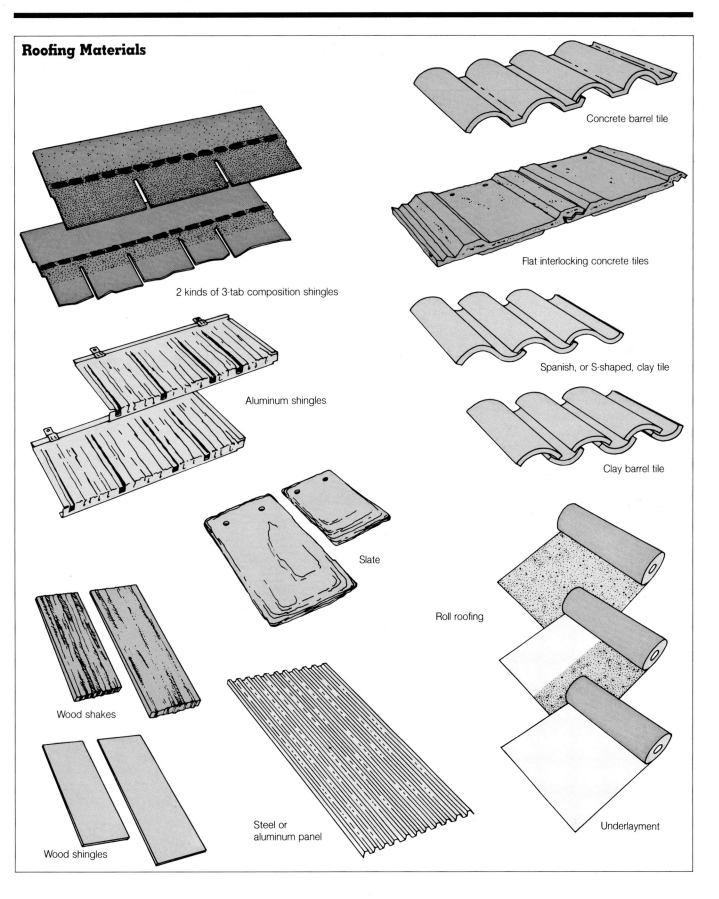

2 kinds of 3-tab composition shingles

Concrete barrel tile

Flat interlocking concrete tiles

Spanish, or S-shaped, clay tile

Clay barrel tile

Aluminum shingles

Slate

Roll roofing

Wood shakes

Wood shingles

Steel or
aluminum panel

Underlayment

cut down, this is no longer true, and they have to be cut from second- or third-growth timber and last only 20 to 25 years. Shakes, with their increased thickness, last longer than shingles. For siding you can use grade 2, which has more sapwood (outer part of the tree) and some knots. Grade 3 has even more sapwood and knots and is undesirable.

Shingles come in lengths of 16 inches, 18 inches, and 24 inches. They are sold in bundles, with four bundles to the square, which will cover 100 square feet at 5-inch exposure.

Shakes are sold in bundles of 18-inch or 24-inch lengths, and in either a heavy- or medium-weight grade. A five-bundle square of 24-inch shakes will cover 100 square feet at 10-inch exposure.

Shingles and sometimes shakes are commonly applied over spaced 1 by 4s or 1 by 6s rather than over a solidly sheathed roof, to allow air circulation (see page 32). This is especially true with shingles, which, because they are machine sawn, fit tightly and smoothly together. Underlayment (see page 34) is always placed under shakes, since their irregular surface allows air to circulate, but is only used under shingles in regions where ice may build up, and then only at the edges of the roof.

Neither shakes nor shingles should be used on roofs with less than a 4 in 12 slope, since they will not readily shed water, and wind can blow rain under them.

The neutral grays and blacks of this compact home are beautifully accented by touches of gleaming brass.

Roll Roofing

This is essentially the same material as composition shingles. However, it does not last nearly as long, because there is only one layer over a roof, while the overlapping of shingles means that there are actually three layers of material on the roof.

There are two basic types of asphalt roll roofing: mineral surface and selvage edge. Underlayment, an asphalt-impregnated paper that is used as a protective bottom layer for many different types of roofs, is also a type of roll roofing.

Mineral-Surface Rolls

These are similar in color and appearance to composition shingles. Mineral-surface roofing is commonly called 90-pound felt because one roll, which covers one square, weighs 90 pounds. It comes in rolls 36 inches wide and 36 feet long, which totals 108 square feet; but because of overlaps, the actual coverage is 100 square feet. It can also be used as flashing and is commonly put in valleys under metal flashing.

Selvage-Edge Rolls

Also called split-sheet roofing, these are smooth surfaced on the upper half and mineral covered on the lower half. When the roofing is applied, the mineral-covered surface overlaps all the smooth surface of the strip below. This overlap provides excellent protection on very low-slope roofs. Two rolls cover one square. Each roll weighs 55 to 70 pounds.

Underlayment

This is the term for the asphalt-impregnated roofing felt used with such roofing materials as composition shingles, shakes, and tile. These rolls are classified by weight per square, with the most widely used type being 15-pound felt (that is, the material to cover one square weighs 15 pounds) and the heavier 30-pound felt. One roll covers either two squares or four, depending on the size of the roll.

Clay and Concrete Tiles

For years the curved clay tiles used on the Spanish missions of California were the standard when it came to a clay tile roof. Strong, beautiful, and heavy, they lasted as long as the house. But they weigh more

Coordinating Colors

For a harmonious exterior, the color of the roof should complement that of the siding. This chart, taken from information provided by the Asphalt Roofing Manufacturers Association, offers some suggestions for appropriate color combinations.

Siding Color	Roof Color
White	White, black, brown, green, gray, red, beige
Ivory	Black
Beige	Brown, green
Brown	Brown, green, beige
Yellow	White, black, gray, brown, green
Deep gold	Black
Coral pink	White, black, gray
Dull red	Gray, red, green
Light blue	Red
Gray-blue	White
Medium blue	Black, brown
Deep blue	Gray
Light green	White, gray, red, brown, green, beige
Olive green	White, black
Dark green	Gray, green, beige
Gray	White, black, gray, red, green
Charcoal	White

than a thousand pounds per square—even more when wet—and generally require that the house be reinforced to hold the weight. Their popularity is being challenged now by concrete tiles, which are cheaper, easier to install, weigh 750 to 900 pounds per square, and come in a wide variety of colors. They can be barrel shaped, like the mission tiles, flat, ribbed, or S-curved. Some varieties of concrete tile are light enough to go on a standard roof. Each tile is molded with a ridge on the back that simply hooks over spaced sheathing, making them much easier to install than clay tiles.

Tiles are more expensive than composition shingles (but often less than shakes) and more difficult to apply, but they never wear out. If you are considering purchasing tiles, some distributors will send a sales representative to your home to evaluate the roof and recommend any additional framing that may be needed.

Metal Roofs

Aluminum and corrugated steel panels are long lasting and relatively easy to apply. Corrugated steel roofs have been made for more than a hundred years. Although quite inexpensive, steel roofs are heavy and will eventually rust. Aluminum panels are replacing the corrugated steel roofs because aluminum is strong, will not rust, and is easy to transport and cut. Both these roofs are noisy in a rainstorm and downright earsplitting in a hailstorm.

Flat metal sheets joined by a standing seam form the most durable metal roof, but they should be installed by a professional. One brand, manufactured in Sweden, is strong enough to span between rafters without wood sheathing, saving a complete step when building a new roof.

Metal panels are efficient conductors of heat, so they must be well insulated underneath. Steel conducts heat about eighteen hundred times faster than wood, and aluminum conducts heat four times faster than steel. Temperature changes cause aluminum to expand and contract considerably, which can mean that roofing nails not properly and carefully placed will eventually work loose.

Aluminum shingles are increasingly popular because of their fire-resistant qualities and long life. They are expensive—comparable in price to shakes—but will last the life of the house. They may be dented by hail. Aluminum shingles are difficult to apply correctly, so you should have them installed by a professional.

Tar and Gravel

This kind of roof is used primarily on structures ranging from flat to a 4 in 12 slope.

Often called a hot-mopped or built-up roof, it is made of alternating layers of underlayment and hot tar, with a protective final coat of fine gravel.

When a tar and gravel roof becomes worn, usually in less than 15 years, another one can be put directly over it, to a maximum of three roofs.

If your house is in need of a built-up roof, the job should be done by professionals. The tar is heated and must be kept at a certain temperature: too cold and it won't spread; too hot and the tar pot can explode.

Cold-Mopped Roofing

This type of roofing is an inexpensive—and much less effective—method of applying a built-up roof. The material is a liquid with an asphalt base. It does not have to be heated because it lacks the clays and other hardening agents that are part of a hot tar roof. Cold-mopped roofing is little used today except for repair work; standard roofing materials, such as composition shingles, shakes, or wood shingles, which can be applied by the homeowner, are better choices.

Slate

Slate roofs are expensive and heavy but will last a lifetime or more. If your roof wasn't originally designed to handle the weight of a slate roof, you will have to call a contractor or architect to reinforce your roof support structure. Slate makes a beautiful roof and is fireproof, but because of its weight it should be professionally installed.

ESTIMATING AND ORDERING MATERIALS

Ordering materials for a roof also means ordering starter strips, drip edges, valley flashing, and hip and ridge shingles or tiles. Plan carefully so that you will not find yourself in the middle of a project and short of materials.

Calculating Roof Area

Basically, square footage is found by multiplying length times width. A shed roof that is 10 feet wide and 12 feet long is 120 square feet. To calculate a simple gable roof, just measure and calculate the square feet on both sides of the roof and then add them together.

If you have a fairly simple roof that you can readily walk around on, just take exact measurements. Many roofs, however, are not simple; in addition, it may be difficult to clamber about them taking measurements. If this is the case, roof estimations may be done from the ground. Measure the roof as if it were projected flat upon the ground, then correct for the amount of slope in the roof by using the area/rake conversion chart.

Using the house illustrated on page 25 as an example, first measure the outline of the house from eave to eave in order to include all the roof overhangs. Transfer these measurements to a piece of paper, then put in the ridge and all the dormers, porch extensions, and chimney.

On paper, you now have a roof outlined as if it were flat. But since it is sloped, it actually covers much more area than it

would appear to on your outline. The main part of the house roof, with a 9 in 12 slope, has two different sections, one narrower than the other. On a strictly horizontal plane, the two areas are as follows.

$26' \times 30' = 780$ square feet
$19' \times 30' = 570$ square feet
Total: 1,350 square feet

Next you must deduct the chimney and the triangular area of the ell roof that projects into the main roof.

chimney: $4' \times 4' = 16$ square feet
ell roof: $\frac{1}{2}(16' \times 5') = 40$ square feet (triangular area)
Total: 56 square feet

Deducting that from the gross area of the main roof leaves 1,294 square feet. For the total on the 6 in 12 roof:

$20' \times 30' = 600$ square feet
$\frac{1}{2}(16' \times 5') = 40$ square feet
Total: 640 square feet

The dormer can be calculated separately; but unless you have many of them, just include it as part of the gross roof area and your calculations will be close enough. If you have any skylights, deduct that area from the total.

In this example there are 1,294 square feet in the main roof and 640 in the ell roof. Using the area/rake conversion chart below to determine the conversion factor, you then multiply the total number of square feet times the conversion factor. For the 9 in 12 roof:

1,294 square feet $\times$ 1.250 = 1,617.5 square feet

For the 6 in 12 roof:
640 square feet $\times$ 1.118 = 715.5 square feet

That makes a total of 2,333 square feet. Add 10 percent for waste, for a total of 2,566.3 square feet. Divide that by 100 and you find that you need 25.6 squares. Make it 26 squares so you will have some on hand for repairs if necessary.

Measuring Special Dimensions of the Roof

A two-dimensional drawing cannot portray a three-dimensional area with absolute accuracy. Sloped lines will actually be longer than the drawing would seem to indicate. You can use conversion charts to calculate the actual dimension of a sloped line.

Eaves and Ridges

These are horizontal and can be measured directly, without using a conversion chart.

To measure the rakes, first use the drawing to find the horizontal distance. Now multiply that times the conversion factor in the chart, depending on the slope of the roof. Add the length of the rakes to the eave measurements to find the total drip edge needed.

Hips and Valleys

These involve sloped distances, so another chart (below) must be used to find their true distances. Find the horizontal distances of hips and valleys on your drawing by noting how far they extend into the roof (for example, one half, one third). Then, using the overall

Hip and Valley Conversion

Slope*	Hip/Valley Factor
4	1.452
5	1.474
6	1.500
7	1.524
8	1.564
9	1.600
10	1.642
11	1.684
12	1.732

* inches per foot

Area/Rake Conversion

Slope*	Rake/Area Factor
4	1.054
5	1.083
6	1.118
7	1.157
8	1.202
9	1.250
10	1.302
11	1.356
12	1.414

* inches per foot

How to Calculate Roof Area

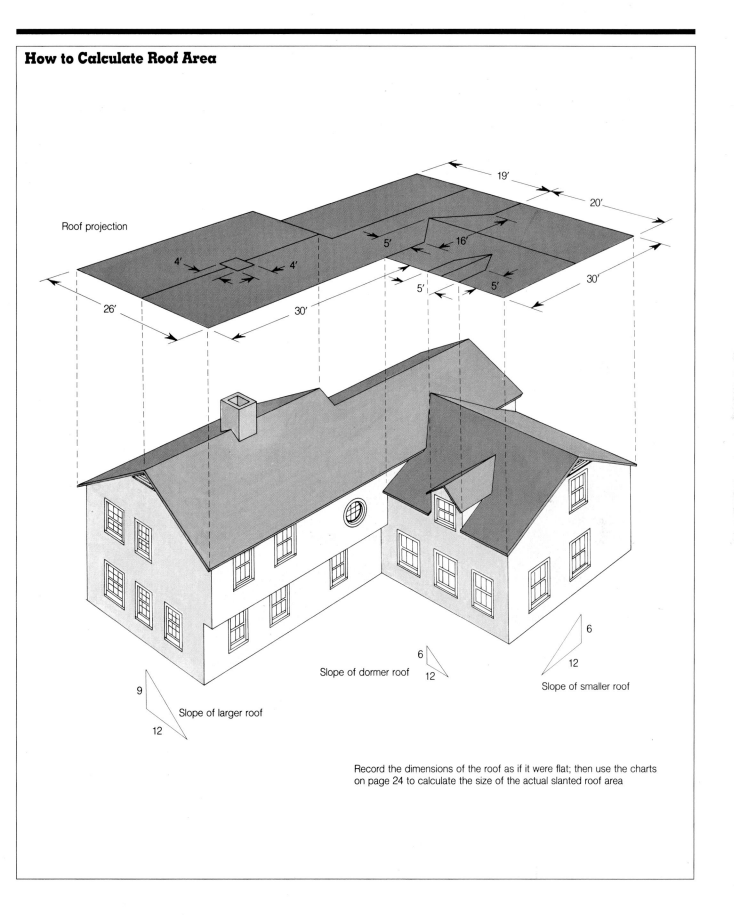

Roof projection

19'
20'
5'
16'
4'
4'
5'
30'
5'
5'
26'
30'

6
Slope of smaller roof
12

6
Slope of dormer roof
12

9
Slope of larger roof
12

Record the dimensions of the roof as if it were flat; then use the charts on page 24 to calculate the size of the actual slanted roof area

Modern equipment can reach second-story roofs easily and make one of the hardest parts of the job a pleasure to watch.

width of the roof, make a close estimate in number of feet. Multiply that by the conversion factor for the appropriate roof slope.

From these figures, your roofing supplier can give you the proper lengths of valley flashing and quantities of ridge and hip shingles or tiles.

Additional Materials

Measure the size of all vent pipes and buy the metal and neoprene rubber flashing units that slip over them.

If flashing is needed around a chimney or skylight, measure the linear amount needed.

You will need roofing cement, which comes in tubes as well as 1-gallon and 5-gallon quantities. For a 1,500-square-foot roof, you would use about 2 gallons of roofing cement. If you don't use it all, seal it tightly; it will last for years and is excellent to have on hand for emergency repair.

For nails, allow 2½ pounds per square for composition shingles, 2 pounds for wood shingles, shakes, or tile.

Be prepared for rain. Make sure that you have some rolls of 6-mil plastic on hand to spread over the roof, and 1 by 4 boards to tack down the edges of the plastic to prevent its being ripped away by wind.

For composition shingles you also need what is called a starter roll. This mineral-coated asphalt roofing material comes in a roll about 8 inches wide (wider rolls are available, and in heavy-snow areas may be required) and is nailed down at the edge of the eaves and then shingled over. It provides needed roof protection under the first row of shingles. On wood shingles and shakes, instead of using a starter roll, the first course is doubled. For roll roofing and for metal and vinyl panels, no starter course is required.

How to Arrange A Delivery

Once you have a list of your estimated material needs in hand, contact several different roofing suppliers to determine the cost of materials and the delivery charges. You should try to arrange delivery as close as possible to when you'll need the materials for installation. In this way you can avoid having to store them for an extended period of time.

If storage is required, try to store the materials inside where they will stay dry and avoid temperature extremes. If this is not possible, store the materials on 2 by 4s to keep them off the ground. Use plastic sheeting to cover the materials in case of rain.

When you order the materials, ask about having them delivered directly on the roof. Roofing suppliers generally have special trucks that are designed for rooftop deliveries.

This will cost more, but the extra cost is offset by the time and hard work required to get the materials on the roof. Carrying materials up a ladder one bundle at a time is not only difficult, it can be dangerous.

If a rooftop delivery is not possible or practical, you can rent a mechanical hoist from a tool supply rental company. Some roofing supply companies have a pulley system available that you can use to transfer materials from the ground to the roof. By attaching the pulley to a ladder, you can lift the materials with a rope. As you bring the bundles up the ladder to the roof, be sure to distribute them along the ridge to spread the weight evenly. If rain is threatening, cover materials with tarps as you stack them. This way you can uncover just the stack you are using, and if the rain does start, you can get off the roof in a hurry without having to worry about your supplies.

ROOFING TOOLS

Fortunately, roofing does not take a lot of expensive or unusual tools. You can probably get the job done with what you currently have in your workshop. But, as with most jobs, roofing is much more enjoyable if you have the right tools. Remember that roofing is more than just nailing down shingles. Maybe the old roof has to be removed first. Then there are drip edges, flashing, gutters, and downspouts to be put on. Here are some tools useful in a roofing job.

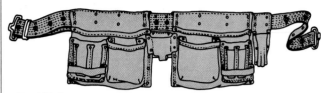

Tool Belt

A standard carpenter's tool belt has 4 pockets for holding different-sized nails and several loops for holding such things as a tape measure and hammer. A tool belt is a time saver, because all your equipment is readily at hand and moves when you do.

Prybar

This heavy metal bar is useful when removing nails and wood shakes or shingles from a roof

Aviation Snips

These are needed to cut flashing and metal drip edges to length

Chalk Line

This tool has a string wound in a container full of chalk. When stretched tight and snapped, the chalk-coated string leaves a straight line over a distance of up to 100 feet. Chalk lines are snapped periodically to keep shingle courses properly aligned.

Chisel and Saw

For removing and repairing any problem areas in the roof sheathing

Tape Measure

A retractable steel tape at least 16 feet long (preferably 25 feet) is needed for installing a neat and professional-looking roof

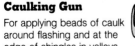

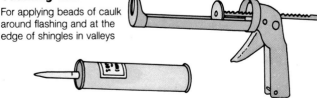

Putty Knife

A putty knife can be used to apply roofing cement around vents. However, the tail of an old wood shingle works just as well and can be thrown away when you're finished.

Caulking Gun

For applying beads of caulk around flashing and at the edge of shingles in valleys

Roofer's Hatchet

Although you can get by with a hammer, the specifically designed roofer's hatchet is well worth the cost. There are two basic types available. A style commonly found in hardware stores has a combination hammer and hatchet for splitting wood shingles or shakes. The hatchet side has a series of holes ½" apart that accept a knurled knob. This creates a shingle exposure guide on the hatchet.

Measure from the hammer face to the hole of your choice, depending on how much shingle exposure you want (see illustration), and screw in the knob. Professional roofers use a similar hatchet that has a small replaceable knife blade on the hatchet end for cutting composition shingles. Dull blades can be quickly replaced.

How Roof Jacks Work

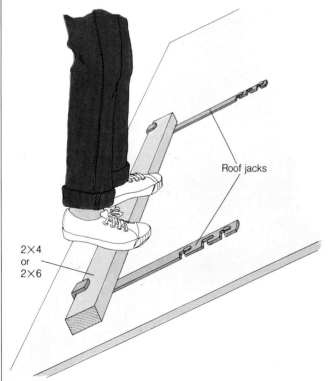

Roof jacks

2×4
or
2×6

Roofing Jacks

These are used on steep or slippery roofs to prevent falling (see page 12). They can be rented.

Power Nailers and Staplers

You can buy a wide variety of power nailers and staplers or rent them from tool rental companies or building suppliers. Most are air operated, requiring the use of an air compressor and hose, although electric-operated versions are offered increasingly by manufacturers. Such tools offer both convenience and increased productivity, especially on assembly-line installation of sheathing and shingles, but some experience is required to use them properly and safely.

Power nailers use nails (up to 16d in size) that have been preloaded in clips, cartridges, or magazines for insertion into the gun. Standard pneumatic staplers will drive staples between 5/16" and 2" long, but staplers used on roofing jobs generally accept staples up to 1½" in length. As with power nailers, the staples are loaded in clips, cartridges, or magazines.

The same factors that determine the size and type of hand-driven fasteners apply to the selection of power-driven fasteners. Your building supplier can give you up-to-date advice on the correct-size fastener to be used for your particular job. Because these tools come in many different designs, be sure to obtain and carefully follow the manufacturer's operating instructions.

A power nailer or stapler is used as follows.
• Load the tool with the desired size of staples or nails.
• Pointing the tool at the ground or away from yourself (and others), connect it to the air supply. The compressed air from your source should be free of dust and moisture. Many tools require an oiler in the air-supply line to keep the tool properly lubricated during operation.
• Check the pressure setting for the correct amount of air pressure or electrical impact. Excessive pressure or impact will drive the fastener through the material and damage its surface.
• Use a piece of scrap stock for practice. This lets you check to make sure that the pressure setting is correct before you begin the actual work. Hold the nose of the tool against the scrap stock and depress the trigger. With the trigger depressed, a fastener is driven each time the nose of the gun is held to the work.

There are several safety precautions to be followed when using power nailers and staplers. First and foremost, be sure to read and follow the manufacturer's operating instructions so that you are familiar with the various safety features of the tool. Wear safety goggles or glasses when operating the tool; always keep its nose pointed toward the work—never aim it at yourself or in the direction of others. When you finish working with the tool, disconnect its air hose or electrical cord before setting down the tool. Never leave it connected when not in use.

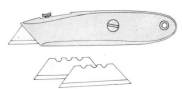

Utility Knife

Choose one that contains several blades that can also be reversed. This knife is most commonly used when cutting composition shingles.

REPLACING AN OLD ROOF

If the existing roof is badly worn or uneven, it's best to remove it. Weight is also a consideration. There are limits to how many layers of roofing a house can bear. The maximum may also be controlled by local building codes. This section will deal with determining whether you can cover your present roof, and if not, how to tear it off.

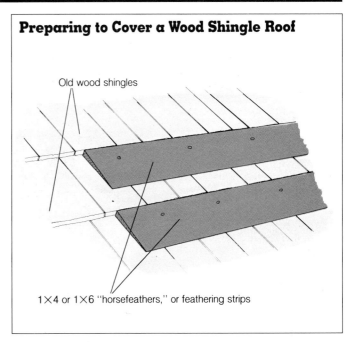

Preparing to Cover a Wood Shingle Roof

Old wood shingles

1×4 or 1×6 "horsefeathers," or feathering strips

Covering An Old Roof

You can apply the new roof directly over the old if certain criteria are met.

Composition Shingles

You can apply a new composition shingle roof directly over the old once you nail down the warped shingles and replace the missing ones. You can apply wood shingles over composition shingles if you first nail on spaced 1 by 4 boards so that air can circulate under the shingles. You can apply shakes directly to a composition roof, since their irregularities allow enough air to circulate. You can apply metal and tile—if your roof is designed to hold the weight of tile—directly over composition shingles. You should not attempt to put roll roofing over composition shingles.

Tar and Gravel

This roof probably has a 4 in 12 slope or less, and that low slope somewhat limits your choices. Since most codes only allow three built-up roofs on a house,

you should first pull off the fascia board along the rake and count the layers of exposed gravel to determine how many roofs are already in place. If there are three already, you must tear them all off before applying any new roof. In most cases you should tear off the old built-up roof anyway—these roofs are usually so uneven that the new roof will also appear uneven.

But if you decide that the existing roof is smooth enough, and it has at least a 3 in 12 slope, you could apply composition shingles over it; just be sure to use roofing nails long enough to penetrate ½ inch into the roofing deck. If the roof has a 4 in 12 slope, you could apply shakes directly, or wood shingles once you have nailed on spaced 1 by 4 sheathing boards. You could also apply a metal roof directly over the tar and gravel. The roof will probably not be strong enough for tile unless you remove the tar and gravel and use lightweight tile. Roll roofing should not be installed over tar and gravel.

Wood Shingles

If the roof is in good condition but not even, you can improve it by nailing beveled strips of

1 by 4s or 1 by 6s against the shingle butts. These strips are called "horsefeathers" or feathering strips. You could then cover the roof with composition shingles, shakes, or metal panels. Before you lay a new wood shingle roof over the old, you should first nail on spaced 1 by 4s to provide good air circulation. Do not put roll roofing over wood shingles.

Shakes

This roof should be torn off. Shake roofs are too irregular to cover with anything new.

Roll Roofing

Assuming slope conditions are satisfied (see pages 18 and 19), you can apply almost any roofing material over roll roofing. Wood shingles require spaced 1 by 4 sheathing boards, and new roll roofing should be put over an old roof only if it is still even.

Tile or Slate

These materials are so long lasting that it's unlikely you'd need to replace them. If you wish to put on a new roof for appearance's sake, remove the old one so as not to overburden the roof supports.

Metal or Vinyl Panels

Always remove panels before applying a new roof.

Roof Condition

In addition to the criteria above, you also must check that your roof is in good condition. Following the instructions on pages 8 to 9, inspect the roof deck for signs of deterioration, which indicates a leaking roof. Go into the attic and look for any signs of moisture or wood rot. If you see any, or if plywood laminations are separating, this must be repaired first. That means pulling off the existing roof.

Outside, check the eaves for wood rot. If you find some here but the rest of the roof appears fine, you can strip off the first two or three courses of shingles, cut out the damaged decking and replace it with matching material, and then shingle over the existing roof.

Inspect the existing roof by going up there or by examining it with a pair of binoculars. Note any loose, broken, or curled shingles. They must be made to lie flat before new roofing can go on. If the existing roof is composed of the old interlocking style of shingle, it will probably be too irregular to cover with any other roofing material.

Replace any broken and missing shingles to provide an even nailing surface. If the drip edges are rusted or broken, remove them and install new ones with the new roof. Any trim boards that are rotten or broken should be replaced.

If you plan to cover wood shingles with composition shingles, inspect for warping, which will make the roof uneven. Warped shingles should be split, then nailed down flat (see pages 102 to 103). Hammer down all protruding nails and replace any missing shingles.

Codes and Permits

Building codes generally stipulate that a residence can have no more than three roofs on it: the original and two follow-ups. Before deciding to put another roof on the old, check how many already exist. You are talking about a lot of weight. Say you have 1,800 square feet of roof to cover with composition shingles weighing 240 pounds per

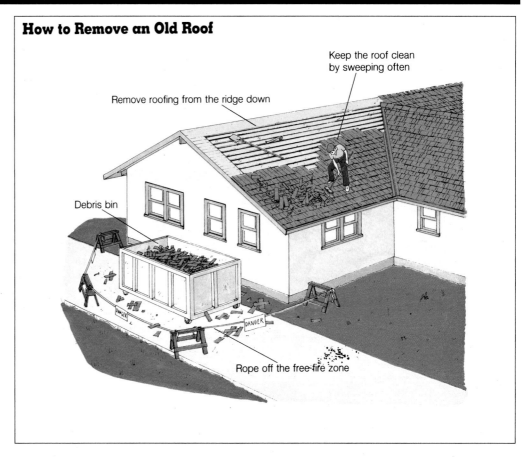

How to Remove an Old Roof

Remove roofing from the ridge down

Keep the roof clean by sweeping often

Debris bin

Rope off the free-fire zone

square. That's 4,320 pounds on the roof. If there are already two roofs on and you add a third, that amounts to 6½ tons of roofing material. It's certainly something to think about during high winds and heavy snowfalls!

Do you need a building permit when adding a new roof or siding? In some areas the answer is no; in others, it's yes. Play it safe and call the building inspection department.

Removing An Old Roof

There is no special trick to removing an old roof, just a lot of hard work.

The primary tool in removing a shingle, built-up, or roll-roofing roof is the flat-bottomed

shovel. Roofing outlets often sell a shovel-like tool that has serrated edges along the tip to cut nails.

Start near the ridge. On built-up roofs use a pick to break open a line along the ridge so that you can get the shovel underneath and begin prying up the material.

On wood shingle or shake roofs, be sure to work your way from the top down, so that debris won't fall through the open sheathing.

With shakes and shingles a crowbar often works better than a shovel. By running the flat end of the crowbar under the shingles, then prying up, you can remove a dozen or more shingles at a time.

Tile can be removed by hand. Slate should be pried up with a crowbar.

To remove metal or vinyl panels, use a crowbar to pry up the panels; pull the nails out.

Removing an old roof creates a large amount of debris. The best way to dispose of it is to obtain a debris box. These come in various sizes and are rented by the week. Have the box placed as close to the house as possible, so that you can dump the material into the box directly from the roof. Having to throw it on the ground and then pick it up again is doing it the hard way. If a debris box is not available in your area, a pickup truck can be used in much the same way, if you don't mind some dents and scratches. Be aware that you are responsible for any cracks in sidewalks and water pipes caused by the weight of the box or the truck that hauls it.

ROOFING ON NEW CONSTRUCTION— ROOF DECKS

There are basically two types of roof decks (or sheathing): solid and spaced. Solid sheathing is plywood, compressed flake boards designated for structural use, or tongue-and-groove material. Spaced sheathing is 1 by 4 or 1 by 6 material. The type of deck needed is determined by the roofing material being used.

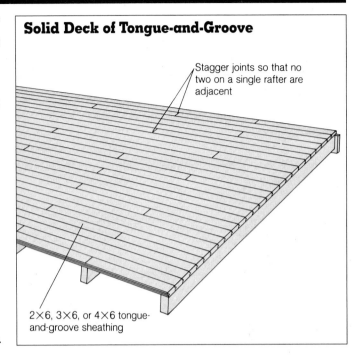

Solid Deck of Tongue-and-Groove

Stagger joints so that no two on a single rafter are adjacent

2×6, 3×6, or 4×6 tongue-and-groove sheathing

Solid Sheathing

In most cases, solid sheathing is used for roofs of composition shingles, roll roofing, and slate.

Starter Board

Also called V-rustic, starter board is commonly used over open eaves and gable over-hangs in place of plywood sheathing, which would look unattractive when viewed from underneath. Starter board is 1 by 6 and similar to shiplap. When using starter board, note that there are two sides to it. The side with the beveled edge goes down, creating the V that shows between boards when they are seen from below.

The first board along the eaves should be carefully aligned along the rafter ends. Snap a chalk line across the rafters to check that they are even. Long lengths of starter board will probably be warped, so it is necessary to push or pull them into a straight line. Each end must fall in the center of a rafter, where it will butt against the next piece.

Carry the boards up about 6 inches past the house wall. Next, cut and nail starter boards up the gable overhangs. Be sure to cut them so that their ends fall in the center of the second rafter, which leaves nailing space for the plywood decking.

Solid Panels

Roofs are commonly covered with 4 by 8 sheets of ½-inch exterior-grade plywood or oriented-strand compressed board. Use the cheapest grade of plywood—called CDX— since it will be covered and appearance is of no importance.

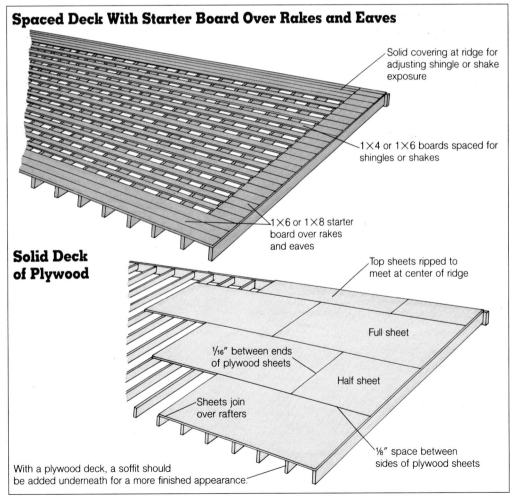

Spaced Deck With Starter Board Over Rakes and Eaves

Solid covering at ridge for adjusting shingle or shake exposure

1×4 or 1×6 boards spaced for shingles or shakes

1×6 or 1×8 starter board over rakes and eaves

Solid Deck of Plywood

Top sheets ripped to meet at center of ridge

Full sheet

1/16" between ends of plywood sheets

Half sheet

Sheets join over rafters

⅛" space between sides of plywood sheets

With a plywood deck, a soffit should be added underneath for a more finished appearance.

The panels run lengthwise across the roof rafters. Align the first panel carefully in the bottom left corner. Double-check that all corners are in line with rafter edges and that the leading edge falls in the center of a rafter, leaving room for the next piece to be butted there.

Nail the bottom course of panels in place first. Use 8-penny (8d) nails spaced every 6 inches along the edges and every 12 inches in the field (middle part of the panel). Plywood will expand and contract depending on its moisture content, so it's important to leave room between panels. The usual gaps are $\frac{1}{16}$ inch between ends and $\frac{1}{8}$ inch between sides; if you live in a very humid area, double these measurements.

Start the second course with a half sheet so that all joints will be staggered. Joints that line up together on the same rafter create a weak roof.

At hips and ridges, nail the panel in place and let it hang over. Snap a chalk line directly over the hip or ridge and then cut the plywood. When you come to valleys, you will first have to measure them, then cut the plywood to fit.

If you are putting on a tile roof, check the manufacturer's instructions. In many cases the plywood is cut back $\frac{3}{4}$ inch on each side of the hip and ridge lines, so that a length of 2-by material can be placed on edge there to support the ridge or hip tiles (see illustration).

Tongue-and-Groove

Made from 2 by 6s, tongue-and-groove boards are used when the roof deck will be visible from inside the house, as in cathedral ceilings. (Thus, with tongue-and-groove sheathing, starter board is not necessary.) The first board should be put down along the eaves with the tongue edge facing toward the ridge. Use a scrap piece about 2 feet long as a hammering block to knock successive boards into place. The tongue-and-groove section should fit tightly together, but leave a $\frac{1}{8}$-inch space at all butt joints for expansion. Put two 16d nails in each board over each rafter. Stagger joints so that they don't all line up on the same rafter.

Spaced Sheathing

Generally made with 1 by 4s, spaced sheathing is most commonly put under wood shingle, shake, tile, and metal panel roofs. On aluminum and corrugated steel panel roofs, 1 by 4s are spaced every 4 feet or according to manufacturer's instructions. On wood shingle roofs the sheathing is spaced the distance of the shingle exposure. Spacing is measured from center to center (abbreviated O.C.). Thus, with a 5-inch shingle exposure, space boards every 5 inches on center. Because 1 by 4s are actually $3\frac{1}{2}$ inches wide, the spacing between boards will be $1\frac{1}{2}$ inches.

On some types of tile roofs, 1 by 6 spaced sheathing is used. The spacing is dictated by the distance from the ridge to the eaves. The manufacturer provides a chart giving exact specifications.

Where appearance is important, either use starter board for the eaves and rakes, or cover

them underneath with a soffit. If eaves are not covered with starter board, position the first three 1 by 4s tightly together to make an ample nailing base for the roofing material.

On shake and shingle roofs, cover solidly about 18 inches on each side of the ridge so that you can make adjustments in the shingle exposure. Use two 8d nails in each board over each rafter.

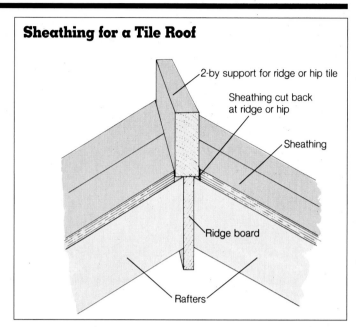

Sheathing for a Tile Roof

2-by support for ridge or hip tile

Sheathing cut back at ridge or hip

Sheathing

Ridge board

Rafters

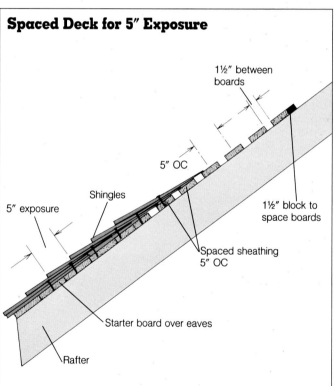

Spaced Deck for 5" Exposure

$1\frac{1}{2}$" between boards

5" OC

$1\frac{1}{2}$" block to space boards

Shingles

5" exposure

Spaced sheathing 5" OC

Starter board over eaves

Rafter

L OADING A ROOF

Wood shingle and shake bundles are light enough that you can carry them up to the roof and stack them as described below. Roll roofing can also be carried to the roof. Loading a roof with heavy composition shingles, however, presents more of a problem.

The best way to load a roof with composition shingles is to have it done by the company that sold you the material. Roofing firms have a special truck they can back up beside the house and raise on hydraulic scissors, run out a steel gangplank, and carry the bundles onto the roof. There is an extra charge for this, but it's well worth it.

If that plan isn't feasible and you have to load the roof yourself, you will have to rent some special equipment. Don't attempt to carry a bundle of composition shingles—which can weigh 90 pounds or more—up a ladder to your roof. It's unsafe and unhealthy.

What you need is a ladder loader, which usually can be found in rental shops. This is an aluminum extension ladder with a series of ropes and pulleys that raise a small platform. Do not exceed the load limit on the ladder, which is generally about 200 pounds. Two people are needed to operate the ladder: one to load the platform and raise it, and the other to unload and stack the bundles.

If worse comes to worse and no ladder loader is available, build a ramp to the roof wide enough for two people to carry a bundle between them.

Bundles of shingles or shakes should be stacked on the roof so that the load is equally distributed and the roofing material is kept out of the way

until needed. To do this, place one bundle lengthwise beside the ridge, and another in the same position on the other side of the ridge. Lay the next three bundles across those two, then the next three across those. Move on now, and start another pile.

Don't leave composition shingles out overnight or in direct sunlight for long (the adhesive strips may melt and fuse). Shingles not being immediately used should be stored off the ground and covered with a tarp or other covering that breathes.

Stacking Tile

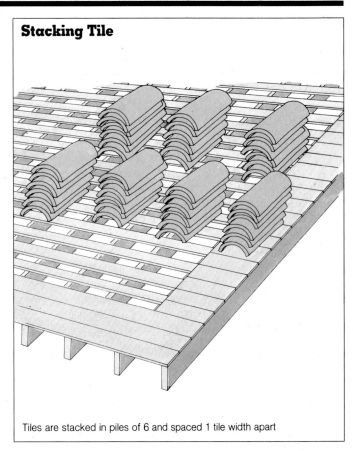

Tiles are stacked in piles of 6 and spaced 1 tile width apart

Stacking Bundles of Shingles

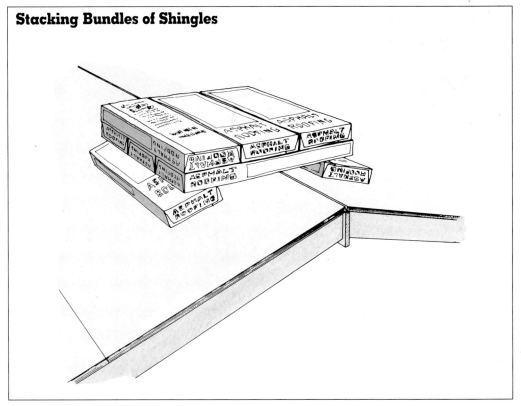

APPLYING UNDERLAYMENT

Underlayment is asphalt-impregnated paper. It is named according to how much one square weighs. Roofers usually work with 15-pound and 30-pound felts.

The roofing manufacturer's instructions usually specify what type of felt underlayment should be used. For composition shingles, one layer of 15-pound felt is best. For shakes, see page 52 for a special technique in applying 30-pound felt. Underlayment requirements for tile vary: Check the manufacturer's instructions. Wood shingles, metal and vinyl panels, and roll roofing take no underlayment.

A standard roll of 30-pound felt is 3 feet wide and 72 feet long. One roll will cover two squares, taking into account a 2-inch overlap, called the headlap, on the top edges.

The felt usually has white lines printed on it. Use those 2 inches from the edge as guidelines for the overlap. Otherwise, you should generally ignore these lines. Keep shingle courses even through measuring and snapping a chalk line, as described on page 45.

It is essential that the felt be laid flat and smooth. Hot sun will soon cause it to buckle, so lay out only as much as you can cover in an hour or so. Don't put felt down over a wet deck or it will eventually bubble and distort shingles.

To lay out felt, align it on the bottom left or bottom right corner of the roof (left-handed people will tend to start on the right) and hold it in place with three roofing nails near the edge, as shown. These nails hold the paper but still allow you to straighten it.

Roll the felt to the other side of the roof, pull it smooth, and cut flush with the rake edge. Making sure it is smooth, put a nail every 3 to 4 feet along the upper half. Do the next layer the same way, overlapping 2 inches at the headlap and 4 inches on the sidelap.

When you reach the ridge, lay the paper across and tack it on the other side. At valleys and hips carry the felt at least 12 inches to the other side and cut. Where a vertical wall meets the roof, such as around dormers, carry the felt up the vertical wall about 5 inches.

When you come to vents, roll the felt next to the pipe and note where the two meet. Cut a slit in the felt, drop the felt over the pipe, then cut the felt around the vent for a smooth fit. When you continue rolling out the felt, check that it was not pulled out of line by the vent pipe.

Here's a tip from the pros: If there are any wrinkles or bubbles in the felt that you can't pull out, make a long cut through the wrinkle and lap the top edge over the bottom. Nail the felt flat.

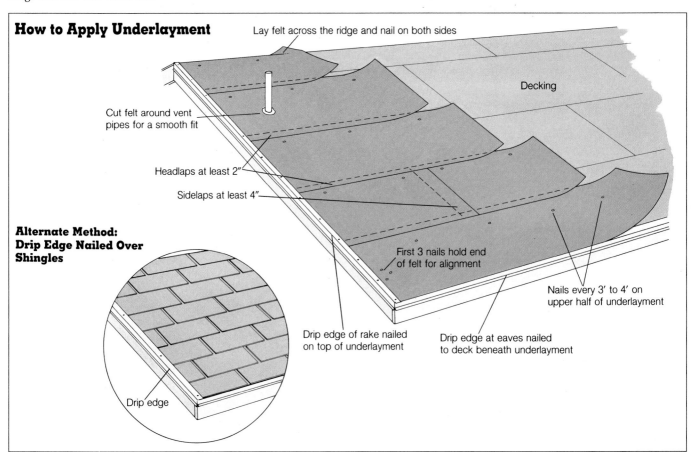

How to Apply Underlayment

Lay felt across the ridge and nail on both sides

Decking

Cut felt around vent pipes for a smooth fit

Headlaps at least 2"

Sidelaps at least 4"

First 3 nails hold end of felt for alignment

Nails every 3' to 4' on upper half of underlayment

Alternate Method: Drip Edge Nailed Over Shingles

Drip edge

Drip edge of rake nailed on top of underlayment

Drip edge at eaves nailed to deck beneath underlayment

NSTALLING FLASHINGS

Flashings protect the roof at those points where water can enter: through broken joints in the roof; wherever something extends through the roof, such as a vent pipe, chimney, or skylight; where two roofs connect to form valleys; or where a roof meets the side of a house, such as with dormers or additions.

Kinds of Flashings

Flashings are generally made of galvanized sheet metal, copper, or aluminum, although valley flashings on asphalt roofs can be made of mineral-surface roll roofing.

The section that follows covers all aspects of flashing except drip edges, which are included in the instructions for installing particular roofs, and skylight flashing, which is described in detail in the section on installing a skylight in Ortho's book *How to Replace & Install Doors & Windows.*

Valley Flashings

There are two basic types of valley flashing: open and closed. Which kind you choose depends on the type of roof you have. Valley flashing is installed prior to installing the roofing material. All kinds of roofs can use open valley flashing. Composition shingle roofs can use open or closed valley flashing. If you have straight valleys between roofs with equal slopes, an open valley that is made of metal flashing is fine. If the valley runs between roofs of different slopes, a full-lace or half-lace closed valley will do a better job.

With open valley flashing, the roofing material stops before the middle of the valley and the special metal sheets installed over the underlayment show through. Metal flashing is commonly used with wood and composition shingles, shakes, or tile. It is called W-metal flashing because it is shaped somewhat like the letter *W*. Made from aluminum or, less commonly, galvanized tin, it comes in 10-foot-long sheets that range in width from 16 to 24 inches. The wide type is used on lower-sloped roofs, particularly those subjected to heavy rainfall. The narrower flashing is used on more steeply sloped roofs in areas that receive moderate to heavy precipitation.

Generally, closed valleys are shingled across only with composition shingles, either fully laced or half laced, over an extra layer of underlayment.

Flashing is needed in the valleys between a dormer roof and a main roof, just as in the main valleys. For composition shingle roofs use the full-lace or half-lace style, as described on pages 36 and 37. For wood shingle, shake, panel, or tile roofs, use W-metal flashing. For roll-roofing roofs use a roll-roofing open valley.

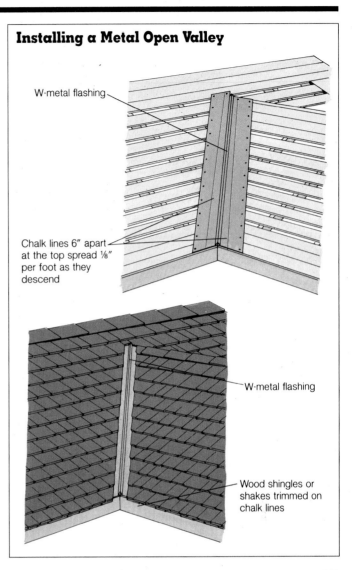

Installing a Metal Open Valley

W-metal flashing

Chalk lines 6" apart at the top spread ⅛" per foot as they descend

W-metal flashing

Wood shingles or shakes trimmed on chalk lines

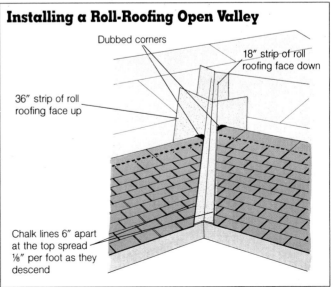

Installing a Roll-Roofing Open Valley

Dubbed corners

18" strip of roll roofing face down

36" strip of roll roofing face up

Chalk lines 6" apart at the top spread ⅛" per foot as they descend

Trim Sharp Corners!

Leaks in valleys are one of the more common causes of leaks in a house. Such leaks sometimes result from the failure to trim—or dub—the sharp corners of shingles where they extend over the valleys.

These sharp corners can act as diverters during heavy runoff and send a course of water great distances across the roof until it begins dripping inside the house.

To dub the corners, lift each shingle and trim back the corner of the one underneath about 2 inches. Now raise and embed the edge of the underneath shingle in a 3-inch-wide bed of roofing cement.

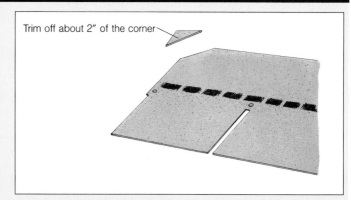

Trim off about 2" of the corner

Metal Open Valley

The valley metal goes on after the roof and valley have been covered with underlayment (see page 34), if necessary. Lay the flashing in place, with the ridge centered up the valley. Use a pair of tin snips and carefully trim the bottom edge even with the edge of the roof along the eaves.

Nail the flashing to the roof deck, placing the nails ½ inch in from the edge of the flashing, every 6 inches. Use aluminum nails with aluminum flashing. (Galvanized roofing nails will react with the aluminum and cause disintegration of both metals.)

If the valley is longer than one length of valley tin, start from the bottom and lap the second length over the lower one by 6 inches. Use tin snips to trim the top flush with the top of the ridge.

In shingling along W-metal valley flashing, first snap chalk lines as trimming guides. At the top, mark 3 inches out from the center ridge on each side. Work down, adding ⅛ inch in width for every foot of valley length. Thus, an 8-foot-long valley would be 1 inch wider at the bottom than at the top.

Calculate the width at the bottom of the valley, then snap the chalk lines. If the valley is especially long, and the bottom marks would fall less than 6 inches from the edges of the valley, move them in to 6 inches. The finish roofing should always cover at least 6 inches of flashing.

As each course arrives at the valley, the top corner of the last shingle must cross the chalk line. If it will fall just a little short, adjust the course farther back. Don't let a joint between shingles fall on the flashing. Also, don't nail into the flashing. Secure the shingle with an extra nail just outside the flashing if necessary.

When you have shingled to the ridge, snap a chalk line on the shingles over the guideline and cut the shingles along the line. Before cementing the shingles over the flashing (do not use nails in the valley), lift each corner and trim off each sharp end. See box above for this important step.

Roll-Roofing Open Valley

Sometimes 90-pound mineral-surface roll roofing is used to flash an open valley. It is generally a little less expensive than the other flashing materials, but it may not last as long as the roof itself.

To use roll roofing for valley flashing, first cut a length of 18-inch-wide roll roofing the length of the valley. Center it, mineral surface down, in the valley, and nail it one side at a time. Then lay a 36-inch-wide strip of roll roofing over it, mineral surface up. Snap a chalk line down its center and position the chalk line over the valley crease. Nail one side first, then bend the strip to seat it securely in the valley, and nail the other side.

Snap chalk lines 3 inches out from the center on each side, diverging ⅛ inch for each foot of descent. Cut the roofing material on these lines as it overlaps the flashing. Trim the corners, as described above, and cement each edge over the valley flashing.

Half-Lace Closed Valley

A half-lace valley may not appear as finished as an open W-metal valley or a full-lace valley, but it can be installed more quickly. It works particularly well where two roofs of different slope are joined.

Carry the shingles from the lower-sloped roof across the valley and at least 12 inches up the other side. Make sure that there are no joints within 10 inches of the center on either side. If necessary, insert one tab between shingles farther back on the course to ensure that the last shingle reaches far enough up the other side.

Now bring the shingles of the steeper roof across to the center of the valley. Snap a chalk line 2 inches back from the center of the valley and trim the shingles along the line with tin snips. Trim all corners (see box above), and cement.

Full-Lace Closed Valley

The full-lace valley is somewhat more time-consuming than the half lace because you must shingle from both sides of the valley at once. On the other hand, you don't have to spend time trimming shingles.

If the roof slopes on both sides of the valley are equal, the full-lace valley is essentially a matter of crisscrossing one course under another as you work on the roof. As with the

Installing a Half-Lace Closed Valley

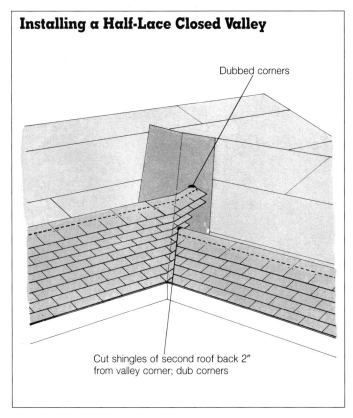

Dubbed corners

Cut shingles of second roof back 2"
from valley corner; dub corners

Installing a Full-Lace Closed Valley

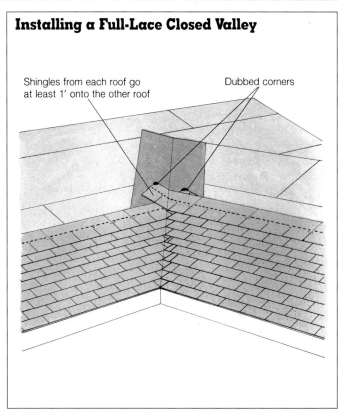

Shingles from each roof go
at least 1' onto the other roof

Dubbed corners

---

half-lace valley, carry the last shingle at least 12 inches up the other side, adding a single tab farther back along the course if necessary, since no joints should be within 10 inches of the valley.

If the roof slopes are different, as in the illustration, two courses of shingles on the flatter roof will cross to the other side before you bring one across from the steep slope. In some cases it may be three to one. You will be able to tell which is necessary as you work.

Vent Flashing

Flashing around vent pipes has become quite straightforward since the arrival of the rubber sleeve. It is widely used on shake, composition, and wood shingle roofs. Vents in tile

roofs are flashed with lead; panel roofs and roll roofing require special approaches.

Composition Shingle, Wood Shingle, and Shake Roofs

The rubber sleeve for vent flashing is a flat piece of galvanized metal with a rubber collar that slips over the vent pipe. Buy the sleeve according to the diameter of the vent, commonly 1½ to 3 inches.

Before putting the sleeve over the vent, bring shingles or shakes up to the bottom edge of the vent pipe. If the top shingle—wood or composition—hits the pipe, notch it to fit. If a course of composition shingles extends well over the pipe, cut a hole in a shingle and slip it over; for shakes or wood shingles, use a keyhole saw to notch two shingles so that they fit

around the vent pipe. Slip the flashing sleeve over the pipe and coat under the metal with roofing cement.

For composition shingles bring the next course across. Where a shingle meets the vent, cut it in a smooth arc about ½ inch away from the pipe. Cutting it too close will allow debris to collect there and possibly dam up water. Embed each shingle that fits over the flashing in roofing cement. Do not use an excessive amount on composition shingles, since it can cause them to blister in the hot sun.

For wood shingles or shakes, choose a broad shake or shingle to go above the vent. For a really fine job, use a keyhole saw to cut an arc to fit the shingle or shake around the pipe. The alternative is to back

that shingle or shake away from the pipe. If the course above the vent pipe is too far away to cover the flashing thoroughly, drop the closest shingle down. It won't be noticed.

Don't forget that the lower edge of the flashing always rides on top of the course of shingles below it.

Tile Roofs

Vent flashing for tile roofs must be made of lead so that it can be molded to the shape of the tile. Apply like standard vent flashing but fill the gap between the flashing and the cutout tile with roofing cement.

Roll Roofing And Panel Roofs

On roofs that do not have shingles or shakes under which the top part of the flashing can slip, you have to improvise. This is the case for panels and roll roofing.

For roll roofing, or for a vent that comes through a flat area of an aluminum panel roof, cut a hole just large enough for the vent pipe. Run the vent pipe through the hole and slip the rubber sleeve flashing over it. Cover the area under the metal flashing with a thick layer of roofing cement and embed the metal in it. Nail through the metal and the roof into cross supports that should have been previously inserted between the rafters. Space roofing nails 2 inches apart all around the edge of the flashing, then cover the edge of the flashing and the nail heads with a smooth layer of roofing cement.

For corrugated metal roofs and fiberglass, you cannot use the flashing sleeve. Pack the opening in the roof and around the pipe with roofing cement. Spread the cement above and around the pipe so that it rises in a smooth sweep from the roof and continues about 3 inches up the vent pipe.

Continuous Flashing

This type of flashing is typically used for vertical walls where a roof meets the front wall of a dormer, or where a shed roof is attached to a wall. Plan the last two or three courses of roofing material before the vertical wall so that the final course, which will go over the flashing, will be at least 8 inches wide. Adjust as necessary. Install the flashing before applying the last course.

The flashing used here is a continuous strip of metal flashing at least 10 inches wide. Use a long straight-edged board to bend the flashing in the middle to match the angle of the roof and wall.

If the vertical wall has not yet been covered with siding, the job is quite simple. Slip the flashing under the felt on the vertical wall and embed the flashing on the roof in a layer of roofing cement. Nail the flashing to the roof but not to the vertical wall. This allows the house to settle at a rate different from that of the attached roof without disturbing the flashing seal.

For aluminum flashing use aluminum nails; use galvanized nails on galvanized flashing.

With the flashing in place and embedded in cement, apply the final course of roofing material and cover each nail head with a dab of cement. When you apply the siding on the vertical wall, do not nail through the flashing.

If the vertical siding is already in place, the flashing must be slipped under it. Gently pry the siding away from the wall and work the flashing up under it. If you run

into nails, notch the flashing to fit around them.

If both the vertical wall and the roof are covered with wood shingles or shakes, the final course on the roof may be too short for a neat appearance.

Instead of using short shakes or shingles, cut a bevel on a length of 1 by 4 redwood or cedar and install as illustrated. The bevel cut will ensure a snug fit under the last course of shingles on the wall.

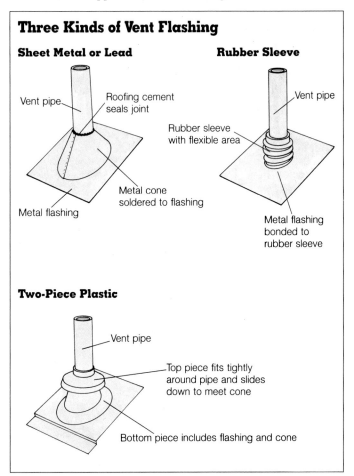

Three Kinds of Vent Flashing

Sheet Metal or Lead

Vent pipe

Roofing cement seals joint

Metal cone soldered to flashing

Metal flashing

Rubber Sleeve

Vent pipe

Rubber sleeve with flexible area

Metal flashing bonded to rubber sleeve

Two-Piece Plastic

Vent pipe

Top piece fits tightly around pipe and slides down to meet cone

Bottom piece includes flashing and cone

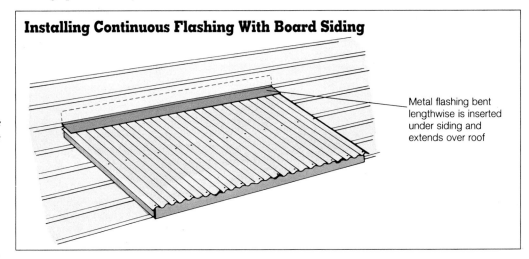

Installing Continuous Flashing With Board Siding

Metal flashing bent lengthwise is inserted under siding and extends over roof

Installing Continuous Flashing With Stucco

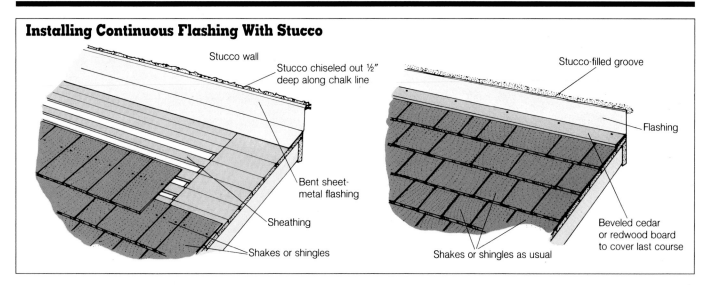

Stucco wall
Stucco chiseled out ½" deep along chalk line
Bent sheet-metal flashing
Sheathing
Shakes or shingles

Stucco-filled groove
Flashing
Beveled cedar or redwood board to cover last course
Shakes or shingles as usual

If the siding is stucco or brick, the flashing must be set into the concrete. The first step is to bend the top ½ inch of the continuous flashing at a 90-degree angle. Do this by clamping the flashing between two boards placed in a vise, and bending it.

Snap a chalk line across the stucco wall about 5 inches up from the roof and use a cold chisel to remove the stucco at least ½ inch deep along the line. On a brick wall, chisel out the mortar between the bricks about 5 inches up from the roof. Bend the top edge of the continuous flashing to fit into the groove; bend the flashing horizontally at the middle so that the lower half will fit smoothly on the roof. Fill the groove with mortar or caulk and press the top edge into place. Nail the last course of the roofing material over the flashing on the roof.

Step Flashing

Use step flashing where the sloping sides of a dormer, skylight, chimney, or other wall meet the roof. Each course of shingles is protected by its own flashing "shingle" cut from aluminum or galvanized tin, 10 inches long and 2 inches wider than the exposure. On a composition roof with a 5-inch exposure, for instance, the flashing shingles are 7 inches wide.

You can make your own step shingles or have them made at a sheet-metal shop. To bend your own, cut the strip, then clamp it between two boards in a vise and hammer it over with a rubber mallet, as shown, so that 5 inches will extend up the vertical wall and 5 inches will extend over the roof. The underlayment should extend up the vertical wall about 5 inches.

The step flashing process described below uses composition shingles with a 5-inch exposure as an example. The process is the same for wood shingles, shakes, and tile. (For roll roofing and panel roofs, use continuous flashing.)

To apply the flashing, position the first piece on top of the starter shingle so the bottom edge of the flashing is flush with the bottom edge of the starter course. Nail the flashing to the roof with two nails placed 1 inch from the top. Do not nail any step flashing to the vertical wall.

If the siding is already in place on your house, you will have to pry it away and slip the flashing up under it. Cut notches in the flashing to fit it past siding nails. For brick or stucco houses, cap flashing must be applied over the step flashing as described in the following section on flashing a chimney.

After the first piece of flashing has been applied over the starter course, apply the first shingle course, with its butt end flush with the lower end of the starter course. Measure 5 inches up from the butt of the first shingle and apply the next piece of step flashing with the bottom end along this line. Nail the top, then put the second course of shingles over it with a 5-inch exposure. Continue up the roof.

Flashing A Chimney

This is the most difficult and important aspect of flashing a roof, since many leaks originate around chimneys. Although a careful nonprofessional can do it, call in a contractor if you have doubts.

Chimney flashing consists of aluminum base flashing and cap (or flashing counter) flashing. The two overlap but must not be joined together, since the chimney and house settle at different rates. Start flashing the chimney after you have installed your roof up to the chimney base.

If your chimney is wider than 2 feet, or if you live in an area of heavy snow and ice, you will first need to construct a "cricket" along the up side of the chimney. Cut it from two pieces of ½-inch exterior plywood (see illustration) and apply it to the roof deck. The cricket diverts snow and water that would otherwise build up behind the chimney and possibly cause leaks.

Next, coat the bricks around the chimney base with asphalt sealant. As each piece of base flashing is installed, it is pressed into roofing cement spread on the bricks. Sealant makes the cement adhere properly to the bricks.

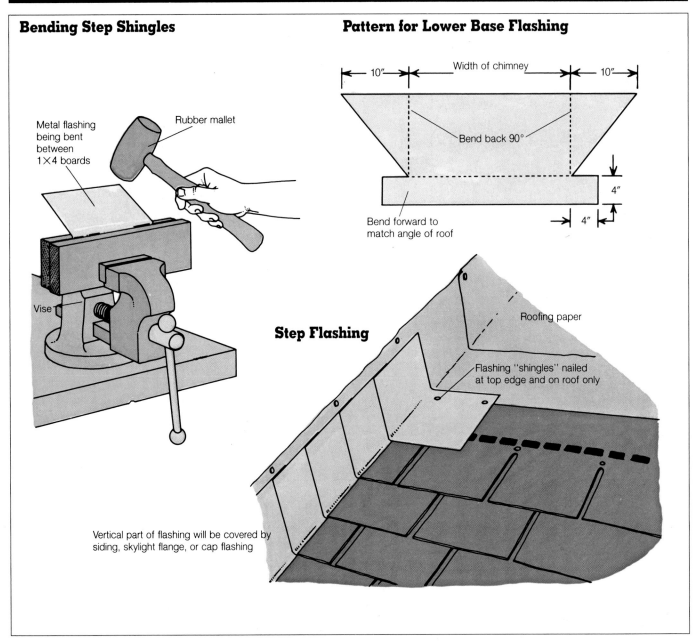

Bending Step Shingles

Metal flashing being bent between 1×4 boards

Rubber mallet

Vise

Vertical part of flashing will be covered by siding, skylight flange, or cap flashing

Pattern for Lower Base Flashing

10"

Width of chimney

10"

Bend back 90°

4"

4"

Bend forward to match angle of roof

Step Flashing

Roofing paper

Flashing "shingles" nailed at top edge and on roof only

Now cut a piece of base flashing for the down side of the chimney, as illustrated, and bend it between two boards in a vise to fit around the chimney. Embed the apron in cement on the roof and press the flanges into cement spread on the bricks. You can hold the flanges in place by driving a couple of nails through them into the mortar. There's no need to remove the nails.

Continue roofing alongside the chimney, applying step flashing as described on page 39. Each piece of step flashing must be embedded in cement against the chimney, and the end of each shingle placed on the flashing must be embedded in cement. Note how the step flashings are cut and bent to fit around the chimney.

Now cut and bend a piece of base flashing to fit around the chimney and over the cricket and at least 6 inches up the side of the chimney, as illustrated. In addition, the base flashing should extend beyond the cricket and onto the roof by 6 inches. Nail it to the roof. This is not necessary if the cricket is large enough—2 feet or longer— to be shingled (in such a case,

shingle it as you would a dormer roof; see page 48).

Now comes the installation of the cap flashing. It should be set in the mortar course two bricks above where the base flashing reaches up the chimney, and extend down to within 1 inch of the roof. Use a narrow cape chisel to remove the mortar between the bricks to a depth of 1½ inches.

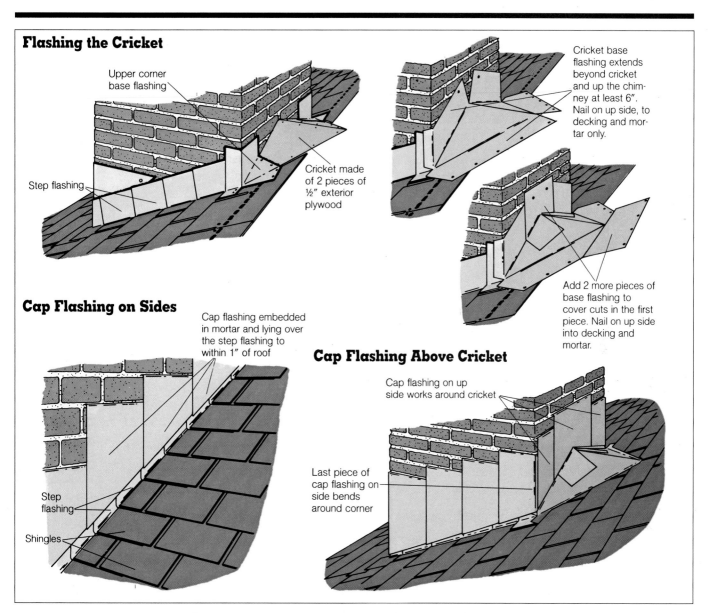

Flashing the Cricket

Upper corner base flashing

Step flashing

Cricket made of 2 pieces of ½" exterior plywood

Cricket base flashing extends beyond cricket and up the chimney at least 6". Nail on up side, to decking and mortar only.

Add 2 more pieces of base flashing to cover cuts in the first piece. Nail on up side into decking and mortar.

Cap Flashing on Sides

Cap flashing embedded in mortar and lying over the step flashing to within 1" of roof

Step flashing

Shingles

Cap Flashing Above Cricket

Cap flashing on up side works around cricket

Last piece of cap flashing on side bends around corner

The first piece of cap flashing is installed on the down side of the chimney. Cut and bend it to fit into the gap you've chiseled out. Pack the joint with portland cement mortar (see box). Cut enough pieces of cap flashing to cover the two sides. Note how the last piece is bent to fit around the corner of the chimney on the up side. Each piece should overlap the next by 3 inches. Cut and fit the cap flashing on the up side of the chimney, working around the cricket.

Mixing and Applying Mortar for Flashing

Cap flashing in a chimney must be held in place with mortar. Make the mix by combining 1 part portland mortar cement to 3 parts fine mortar sand. Three cups of mortar and 9 cups of sand will probably be enough. Put the mix in a bucket, then slowly add water and stir constantly. Add water just until the mixture is the consistency of thick whipped cream. The sand particles should be mixed so thoroughly that they are not visible.

Use a wire brush to scrub out joints where you removed mortar. Wet the joints well, then apply fresh mortar.

Fill the joint with mortar, then insert the flashing strip in the center of the opening. Push it firmly into place. Smooth and press the mortar above the flashing with your finger.

After a couple of hours, wet the mortar with fine spray, then wet it again the following day if you remember. This will help it set slowly and keep it from cracking.

INSTALLING GUTTERS AND DOWNSPOUTS

Gutters are installed on eaves to collect runoff from the roof and channel it into downspouts that direct it away from the house foundation. Without gutters and downspouts, water dripping from the eaves could cause soil erosion or could saturate the soil, then seep into the crawl space or through basement walls.

Selecting Gutters And Downspouts

Gutters and downspouts are most commonly made from vinyl, galvanized metal, or aluminum. Copper and wood gutters exist, but they are more expensive. Vinyl comes in a wide variety of colors. Aluminum and galvanized metal are sold either factory painted or bare, which allows you to paint them to match your house, if you wish.

Gutters and downspouts are sold in 10-foot lengths, which are the easiest to handle; longer ones can be specially ordered. Aluminum gutters are extruded on site, when installed by a contractor, and can be made to any length. Gutter widths are usually 4 inches, 5 inches, or 6 inches.

As a general rule roofs of 750 square feet or less use 4-inch-wide gutters; roofs up to 1,500 square feet use 5-inch gutters; and roofs of more than 1,500 square feet should take 6-inch gutters.

Gutters are sometimes half round but more commonly have what is called a forged shape. Downspouts are either round or square, and are often corrugated, giving them additional strength.

The gutter sections can be hung from the eaves with any of a variety of devices. The spike and ferrule, or the two other styles of brackets, are quite commonly used. Strap hangers provide more support but must be installed before the roof is put on. It is virtually impossible to nail them to a completed roof without damaging the roofing material. Downspouts are secured to the side of the house with galvanized straps.

A new look in downspouts is chains rather than channels. Vinyl-covered, galvanized steel, or brass chains are suspended from the drop outlet to the ground, and water runs down the links. The running water is visible, and imparts a somewhat Japanese feeling.

Estimating Your Needs

First measure the length of all the eaves to calculate the number of gutter sections and supports—one every 3 to 4 feet—you will need. Count the number of inside and outside corners. Figure the number of left and right end caps.

A drop outlet is needed for every 40 feet of gutter, so calculate the number needed. Three elbows are needed for each drop outlet: two to reach the side of the house and one on the end of the downspout. Count the number of downspouts needed and add a few extra to be cut and used as connectors between the elbows at the top. Don't forget the straps for the downspout pipes, one for every 6 feet of pipe.

Now count how many slip connectors you need to join the pipe, and remember that you do not need one where the gutter sections meet at corners or drop outlets.

Don't forget a splash block or leader for each downspout.

Installing Gutters And Downspouts

Gutters should slope about 1 inch for every 20 feet. If you have a run of 40 feet or more, then slope the gutters from the middle of the run and put a downspout at each end.

To lay out the gutter slope, tack a nail to the fascia board at the high end of the slope, measure the run, and drop 1 inch every 20 feet. Tack a nail at this position on the other end of the slope and snap a chalk line between the two points. Use the line as a guide.

Lay out all the components on the ground below the eaves. Measure the gutter runs and note the downspout locations, then cut the gutters accordingly. If the gutters are unpainted metal or plastic, cut them with a hacksaw. Use tin

Gutter Installation

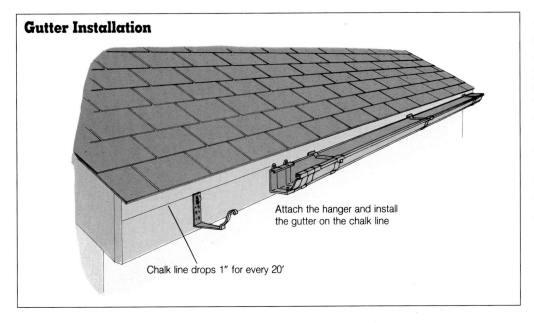

Attach the hanger and install the gutter on the chalk line

Chalk line drops 1" for every 20'

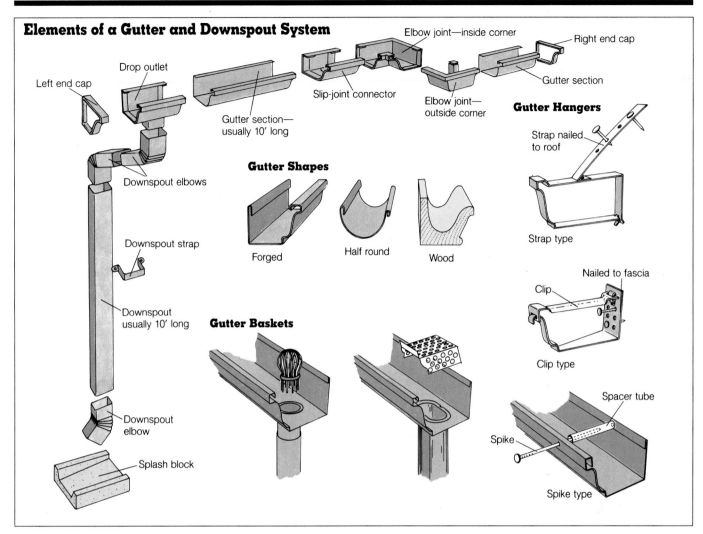

Elements of a Gutter and Downspout System

Left end cap

Drop outlet

Elbow joint—inside corner

Right end cap

Gutter section

Gutter section— usually 10' long

Slip-joint connector

Elbow joint— outside corner

Downspout elbows

Gutter Shapes

Forged

Half round

Wood

Gutter Hangers

Strap nailed to roof

Strap type

Downspout strap

Downspout usually 10' long

Gutter Baskets

Nailed to fascia

Clip

Clip type

Spacer tube

Spike

Spike type

Downspout elbow

Splash block

snips on painted gutters to minimize shattering the enamel paint. To steady the gutters while sawing, slip a length of 2 by 4 in the gutter about 1 inch back from the cut, then squeeze the gutter against the block. Use a file to remove all burrs (jagged edges) from the cut edge.

Gutters should be installed by two people, if possible. One supports the far end while the other installs the gutter and its hangers. If you don't have a helper, hang the far end in a loop of string from the guide nail, then work toward it.

When all pieces are connected and secure, go back and seal each joint with caulk to prevent leaks.

Connect the downspout elbows to the drainpipe on the drop outlet by drilling holes on opposite sides and inserting sheet-metal screws. Connect the elbows to the downspouts in the same manner.

Bend the straps to fit the downspout, then screw them to the siding (the method is the same for all materials). Fit the

elbow on the end of the downspout and put the splash block under it. If you wish to carry the water farther from the house, attach a length of downspout to the elbow. This extension can be buried and run to a dry well, as described below.

Finally, put strainer baskets over the downspout holes and aluminum or vinyl mesh over the gutters. They'll keep out leaves and debris, which can produce clogs. These two items are available wherever gutters are sold.

Installing Dry Wells

If you have trouble keeping roof runoff water diverted from your foundation, you can install dry wells, one for each downspout. These are holes about 4 feet across and 4 feet deep placed 6 to 10 feet from the house. Runoff water from the roof is directed into the dry well, where it can seep deep into the ground.

Bury a length of downspout pipe from the downspout to the well with just enough slope to ensure good water movement. Fill the hole with coarse gravel and replace the sod on top.

43

Applying a composition roof is more than simply nailing on some shingles. Making a good roof involves smooth underlayment, correctly applied drip edges, straight shingle courses, and proper flashing around vents and chimneys and in valleys. All this comes with practice. The secret to a good roof is doing careful work; mistakes mean leaks.

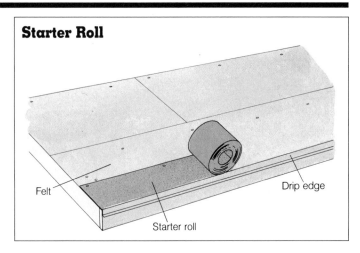

Starter Roll

Felt · Starter roll · Drip edge

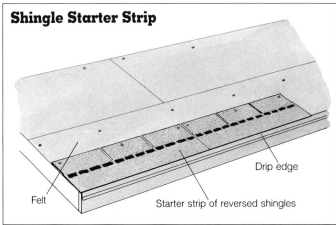

Shingle Starter Strip

Felt · Drip edge · Starter strip of reversed shingles

The following directions apply to all roof types except hip roofs; see page 47 for shingling a hip roof.

Preparations

Before you begin, be sure that you have not only all the shingles you need but also all the various and sundry special items. Running short of drip edges, aluminum nails, or some other small item can be extremely frustrating when you are involved in the actual labor.

Drip Edges

The first item to be put on a new roof is the drip edge along the eaves. Drip edges are L-shaped strips of aluminum or galvanized steel that are nailed along the eaves and rakes of your house to prevent wood rot in the roof-deck edge. Always place the wider side of the drip edge on the roof and let the other end hang over the exposed edge of the roof deck.

Aluminum drip edging should be nailed with aluminum nails. Galvanized roofing nails will cause a chemical reaction that will result in disintegration of both metals.

After drip edges are applied to the eaves (only the eaves, not the rakes), lay the underlayment over the first section of the roof (see page 34).

Drip edges for the rakes may be applied in two different fashions. One style is to put them over the underlayment. An increasingly popular method is to put them over the shingles. This method prevents rain from blowing under the shingle edges.

Flashing

The next step is to install the valley flashing. Follow the instructions on pages 35 to 37; other forms of flashing will be applied later.

Starter Roll

In all types of shingling, an extra layer is always applied along the eaves. This is because shingles in subsequent courses overlap at least once for double coverage, and the first row needs a similar overlap. This layer is applied after the drip edges, underlayment, and valley flashing are in place.

The easiest method of providing the extra layer is to apply a starter roll. This is a 7-inch- or 8-inch-wide roll of mineral-surface roll roofing that is nailed along the eaves. It should overhang the edge of the roof by ½ inch.

If you neglected to buy the starter roll, you can use shingles as a starter course. Just reverse them so that the tabs point up the roof and the upper edge overhangs the eave by ½ inch.

Nailing Shingles

If you are right-handed, always start shingling from the lower left corner of the roof. Curl your left leg under you and use your right leg to maintain your position on the roof. As you shingle you will work up and out to the right. If you're left-handed you'll probably want to reverse directions.

By far the most widely used composition shingle is the three-tab shingle. Each end of the shingle has half a cutout that, fitted against another shingle, forms a full cutout.

Each three-tab shingle is fastened with four roofing nails—one nail an inch in from each end and one nail above each cutout. If the shingle has a self-sealing strip, place nails just below it, not in it or above it.

It is important that the first course of shingles be perfectly straight. To align composition shingles, let the first one overhang the drip edge by ¼ to ⅜ inch and nail it down. Place another shingle the same way at the other end of the roof. Now snap a chalk line between the two along the top edges and line up the top edges of intervening shingles along that chalk line.

Lining Up the First Course of Composition Shingles

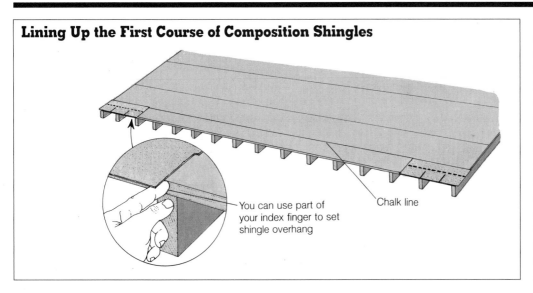

You can use part of your index finger to set shingle overhang

Chalk line

Composition Shingle Nailing Pattern

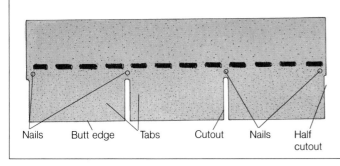

Nails   Butt edge   Tabs   Cutout   Nails   Half cutout

Check for straightness every three or four courses by measuring up from the butts of the shingles at each end of the roof and snapping a new chalk line on which to place the butts for the next course.

Shingles must be cut to fit properly around vents, along the rake, in valleys, and beside flashing. Composition shingles should be cut with a utility knife or with the razor blade in a roofer's hatchet. Always turn over the composition shingle and cut on the back side; cutting on the mineral surface will quickly dull your blade. Score the shingle deeply, then bend it until it breaks.

Shingling Patterns

After the starter roll is nailed on, you are almost ready to start shingling. You now have to choose which shingling pattern you want. The three basic shingling patterns are 6 inch, 5 inch, and 4 inch. The terms refer to the distance each shingle is offset from the one below it to prevent leaks from working through the cutouts. All patterns will protect the roof equally well.

Six-Inch Pattern

This is the easiest style to apply and is the one shown in the directions on the bundles. At the start of each course of shingles, you cut off part of the first

shingle, working in 6-inch increments. The remaining shingles in each course are whole ones. The resulting pattern aligns each cutout directly above another cutout in every other course. There is one problem with the 6-inch pattern in roofs 40 feet or longer: It is difficult to keep the cutouts perfectly aligned up the roof because of inherent minor differences in individual shingles. You can keep them straight, however, by periodically snapping vertical chalk lines on the underlayment as guides, as described below.

Start the 6-inch pattern by nailing a full-length shingle in the bottom left corner. The bottom edge should overhang the eave by ¼ to ⅜ inch and the left edge should be flush with the edge of the rake. Put another shingle at the opposite end of the roof and snap a chalk line between the two along the top edge to make a perfectly straight first course. Nail on the first course.

Now cut 6 inches, or a ½ tab, off the left edge of the first shingle on the second course. Use your hatchet gauge to set the 5-inch exposure at both ends of the shingle and nail it down. (Exposure, or weather, is the distance from the butt of the shingle to the butt of the next shingle above.) For the third course, remove 12 inches, or a full tab, from the first shingle and put it in place. Continue in this manner, removing an additional 6 inches each time, through the sixth course, where you will have removed 30 inches, or 2½ tabs. Carry each course partway across the roof, far enough to keep the pattern going. Start the seventh course with a full shingle and repeat the process. When you get to the ridge, go back and fill out each course across the roof, from the bottom up.

Do not attempt to alternate whole shingles and shingles with a ½ tab removed. This is a guaranteed leaky roof. When starting each course always remove an additional 6 inches. Save the cutoff pieces and use them at the other end of the roof to finish out courses.

To keep the cutouts aligned vertically, snap two chalk lines up the roof on the felt. Put the first one 36 inches in from the edge of the rake (the length of one shingle) and the second one 72 inches in (the length of two shingles). If the roof is interrupted by a dormer, chalk lines must also be snapped on the other side of the dormer to keep the pattern consistent. The process of working around a dormer—tying-in—is explained on pages 48 to 49.

Five-Inch Pattern

This pattern is widely used by professionals, because the 5-inch increments are the same as the exposure. This so-called random pattern also eliminates the problem of aligning vertical cutouts on long roofs.

The first course begins with a full-length shingle. The second course begins with 5 inches removed from the left end. There is a trick to doing this work quickly. After the first shingle is down, put the second-course shingle on top of it, then use the hatchet gauge to move it 5 inches to the left of the first shingle. Grasp the overhanging portion right at the rake edge, flip the shingle over, and cut it. Put the cut shingle back in place and use the gauge to adjust the exposure at each end and the distance from the end of the first shingle. Nail it down. Always set the shingle according to the hatchet gauge, not the cut end, which may be slightly inaccurate. When the roof is complete, you can trim the edge more precisely or cover it with a drip edge.

The third course is done in the same manner, offsetting it from the second course by 5 inches, which results in a total of 10 inches taken off that shingle. Continue in this manner through the seventh course, from which you remove 30 inches. Taking 5 inches off the eighth course would leave only 1 inch of shingle, which is too little to work with. Start the eighth course with a full shingle and continue.

Keep working up the roof, filling out each course only far enough to keep the pattern going. Cutting and laying shingles along the rake while you work up the roof is the slow part, but do it accurately. When you reach the ridge, go back to the eaves and start filling out each course, working from the bottom up.

Every three or four courses, check that your work is not drifting out of line. Do this by measuring from the butt ends of the first course at each end of the roof up to any given course. The measurements should be the same. If one course has drifted, snap a chalk line to straighten the next course. Don't remove a crooked course unless it is radically out of line, since it will not likely be noticed.

Four-Inch Pattern

This style is needed only on low-slope roofs with slopes such as 2 in 12 or 3 in 12. In these cases the underlayment should be overlapped by 19 inches instead of the standard 2 inches, for extra protection against leaks.

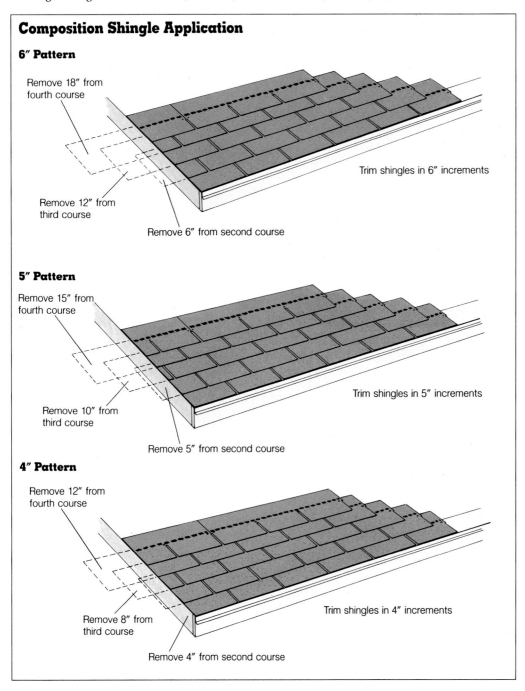

Composition Shingle Application

6" Pattern

Remove 18" from fourth course

Remove 12" from third course

Remove 6" from second course

Trim shingles in 6" increments

5" Pattern

Remove 15" from fourth course

Remove 10" from third course

Remove 5" from second course

Trim shingles in 5" increments

4" Pattern

Remove 12" from fourth course

Remove 8" from third course

Remove 4" from second course

Trim shingles in 4" increments

Applying Hip Shingles

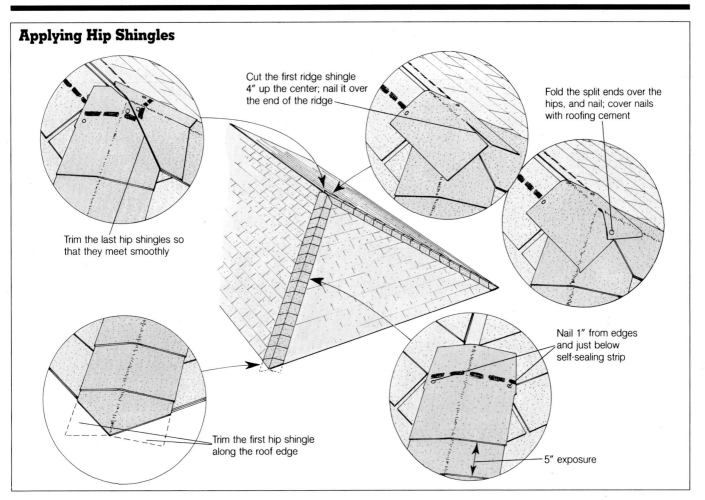

Cut the first ridge shingle 4" up the center; nail it over the end of the ridge

Fold the split ends over the hips, and nail; cover nails with roofing cement

Trim the last hip shingles so that they meet smoothly

Nail 1" from edges and just below self-sealing strip

Trim the first hip shingle along the roof edge

5" exposure

As with the other patterns, start the first course with a full shingle, then trim the first shingle in each successive course in 4-inch increments. Continue through the ninth course, from which you will remove 32 inches. The tenth course starts with a full shingle.

Don't try a 3-inch pattern just to be different—there should never be less than 4 inches between cutouts in any two courses.

Shingling a Hip Roof

A little more cutting is required for a hip roof. Start in the lower left corner if you are right-handed (if you are left-handed, start in the lower right corner) and place the starter course and

first course as you would on a standard roof, but along the hip, cut the shingle with no overlap. Start the second course in standard fashion, cutting the shingle on the line of the hip.

Before applying the hip shingles, tack a strip of window flashing over the hip as added protection against rain.

Hip Shingles

Since ridge shingles cover the top of the last hip shingle, hips should go on first. You can either make your own hip shingles by cutting them from full shingles, which is tedious, or you can buy them ready-made. If you cut your own, cut

as illustrated for a really smooth fit. Put the first shingle in place at the eave, then trim along the roof edge, allowing a ½-inch overhang. Then tack a hip shingle temporarily in place at the top. Snap a chalk line between the top and bottom along one edge to keep the hip shingles straight. Remove the top shingle. Apply the hip shingles from bottom to top, putting the nails 1 inch in from the edges just below the self-adhesive strip. Use the hatchet gauge to give each hip shingle a 5-inch exposure.

Do the same on the other hips until you reach the ridge. Trim the last hip shingles so that they will meet smoothly in the center rather than overlap

(see illustration). Now cut a ridge shingle (they are the same as hip shingles) about 4 inches up the center, fit one split end over each hip, and nail down. Cover each nail head with a dab of roofing cement.

Ridge Shingles

Generally, ridge shingles should be applied with the exposed ends facing away from prevailing winds. However, for a hip roof, start from the hips and work toward the center. For either type of roof, put a shingle in place at each end and snap a chalk line along one edge to keep the shingles straight. Use a 5-inch exposure and put nails 1 inch from the edges and just below the self-adhesive strip.

When shingles meet in the center, trim the final shingle to fit, then cap the joint with a shingle that has had the top portion trimmed off. Nail at each corner and cover the nail heads with roofing cement.

When shingling a ridge from one end to the other, the last shingle should be trimmed and capped in the same way.

Shingling A Dormer Roof

Dormer roofs should be shingled when the courses on the main roof reach the eaves of the dormer roof. They are shingled in a standard manner, and the valleys are protected by either a full-lace or a half-lace valley, as previously described.

Dormer ridge shingles should be applied before you carry the main roof shingles across above the dormer ridge. When applying ridge shingles to a dormer, start from the outer edge and work toward the main roof. When you reach the main roof, split the top of the shingle and carry it at least 4 inches up the main roof. Shingles coming across on the main roof should lap that junction.

Tie-Ins

Tying-in a roof is the process of working around a dormer so that the cutouts between the tabs are vertically aligned, without a break, on both sides of, and above, the interruption caused by the dormer.

To do this, shingle up the roof toward the ridge while at

the same time extending the courses toward the dormer. Meanwhile, carry the lower courses beyond the far side of the vertical dormer wall. As you reach the dormer roof, shingle it first, then bring the main roof shingles over to it and complete the left-side valley, as described on pages 35 to 36.

Now for the actual tie-in: Carry the course immediately in line with the top of the dormer roof to a point about four shingles beyond the right side (left side, if you're left-handed) of the dormer roof. Nail only the tops of the shingles so that the course that is eventually brought up to it can be slipped underneath.

Continue roofing above this line all the way to the ridge. Now, using the cutouts in these upper courses as guidelines, snap a chalk line from the ridge to the eave near the right edge of the dormer. Move over 36 inches and snap another chalk

line. Use these as guidelines as you bring the shingle courses up the right side of the dormer. Slip the tops of the last course under the tabs of the course that is in line with the top of the dormer roof. Generally, as you reach the right side of the

Cutting Hip Shingles

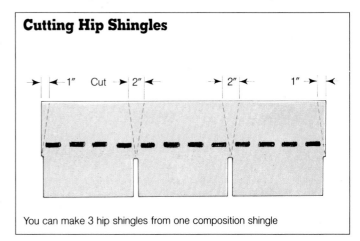

You can make 3 hip shingles from one composition shingle

Ridge Shingles on a Hip Roof

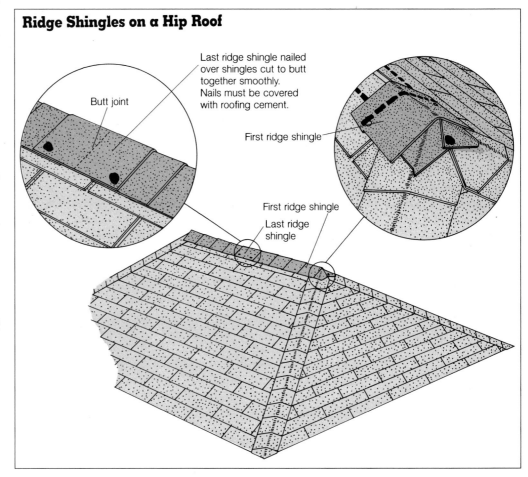

Last ridge shingle nailed over shingles cut to butt together smoothly. Nails must be covered with roofing cement.

Butt joint

First ridge shingle

First ridge shingle

Last ridge shingle

dormer, you will have to cut a shingle an irregular amount so it fits against the dormer wall and the cutout is in line with the chalk line. The second chalk line 36 inches away is a means of double checking your work.

It's a good idea to snap horizontal lines across the roof on the right side of the dormer to keep that side aligned.

When measuring from the eaves for these horizontal lines, be sure to add the amount of shingle overhang at the eaves.

New Roofing Over Old

Roofing over an existing roof adds insulation, eliminates the need for underlayment, and saves you the time and trouble of tearing off the old roof. But if you feel that the old one is too irregular for a smooth new finish, tear it off. You are going to live with the new one 20 years or more and you will want it done right.

Covering Composition Shingles

Any irregularities in the existing roof must be repaired in order to produce a smooth roof. Any warped or bent composition shingles should be split and nailed flat. Missing shingles must be replaced so there won't be a sag in that spot.

When covering an existing roof of composition shingles, it is easiest to match the shingling pattern already used on the old roof.

The first step in roofing over an existing asphalt roof is to apply a starter strip along

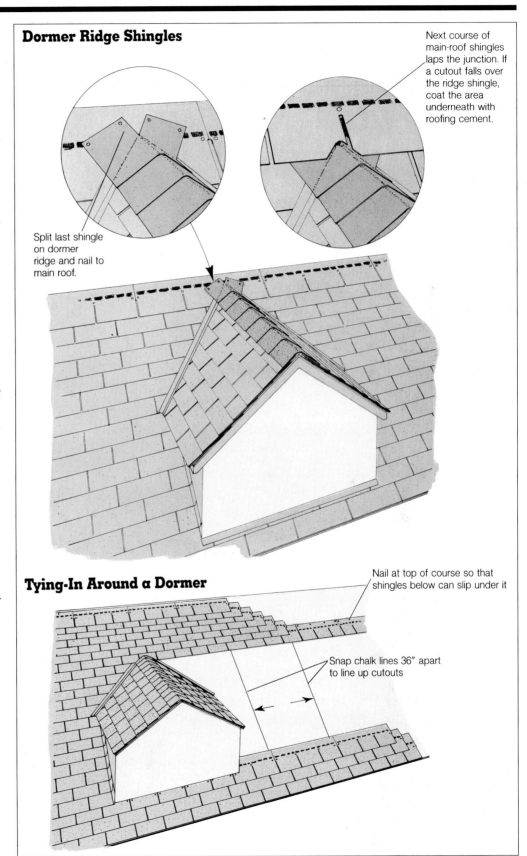

Dormer Ridge Shingles

Next course of main-roof shingles laps the junction. If a cutout falls over the ridge shingle, coat the area underneath with roofing cement.

Split last shingle on dormer ridge and nail to main roof.

Tying-In Around a Dormer

Nail at top of course so that shingles below can slip under it

Snap chalk lines 36" apart to line up cutouts

the eaves. Measure the shingle exposure on the existing roof (commonly 5 inches or 6 inches). Using the new shingles, make the starter strip that width. Cut the shingles to match the exposure in the old roof, and nail the first one with the adhesive strip adjacent to the eaves, as illustrated. If the existing shingle does not extend far enough out to spill water into the gutter, cut the starter shingle wide enough to do so. Cut enough starter shingles to go along all the eaves. Discard the tab ends.

On a 5-inch exposure roof, remove 2 inches from the top of a shingle and butt it up against the bottom of the third course of existing shingles. This 10-inch-wide shingle covers the starter course and the second course on the old roof. Cut enough of these 10-inch-wide shingles to run the length of the eaves.

For a 6-inch exposure, apply a full shingle to cover the 6-inch-wide starter strip and the second course. For wind resistance, put a dab of cement under each tab of this first course.

Now cut 5 inches or 6 inches—depending on the shingling pattern on the old roof—off the rake side of the next shingle and butt it up against the bottom of the fourth course of existing shingles. You will note that this second course leaves only a 3-inch exposure on the first course. This is not a problem, because in most cases it cannot be seen from the ground.

For all remaining courses, cut and apply just as you would for a new roof. The exposure follows automatically, since all new shingles are butted up against existing courses. Remember to use 1¾-inch nails.

Covering Tar And Gravel

As explained on page 29, it is preferable to remove the built-up roof. However, if you prefer to roof over it, follow the instructions above.

Covering Wood Shingles

The directions for covering composition shingles also apply to covering wood shingles.

Shingling an Extrasteep Roof

A roof is considered extrasteep if it is 60 degrees or more, or 21 in 12. The problem is that the self-adhesive strip does not function properly on such steep roofs.

To correct this, apply a quarter-sized spot of roofing cement under each tab and press in place. Do not apply in excess or the shingle may blister.

Actually getting the bundles up onto the roof is the hardest job and should be contracted as part of the delivery, if possible. Be sure and stack them over the ridge as shown on page 33.

INSTALLING A SHAKE ROOF

Shakes come in 18-inch, 24-inch, and 32-inch lengths and in medium and heavy grades. There are three basic types: taper-split, hand-split and resawn, and straight-split. The first two types are thick at the butt and taper to a thin top. Straight-split shakes are equal in thickness throughout their length and are too bulky to be suitable for residences.

Some General Guidelines

Common exposures for shakes are 7½ inches for 18-inch shakes, 10 inches for 24-inch shakes, and 13 inches for 32-inch shakes. These exposures provide the standard two-ply coverage, which means giving 24-inch shakes a 7½-inch exposure, and 18-inch shakes a 5½-inch exposure.

As a general rule, shakes function best on roofs with at least a 6 in 12 slope, particularly in wet and humid climates.

Shakes are always nailed down with only two nails,

regardless of how wide the shakes may be. Place the nails about ¾ inch from the edges and 1 to 2 inches above the exposure (the distance from the butt of the shake to the butt of the shake above). The exposure, also called weather, varies depending on what type of shake you are using and the slope of your roof. Set the exposure with the help of the gauge on the roofer's hatchet. Always check the weather at both ends of the shake to keep your courses straight. Always nail in the same direction—from left

to right if you're right-handed, right to left if you're left-handed. If you see that a shake is crooked, don't try to realign it after two nails are in it. It will only buckle or split. Take out the nails and do it right.

It is important that the first course of shakes be straight. To align, let the first one overhang the drip edge by ¼ to ⅜ inch and nail it down. Place another shake the same way at the other end of the roof. Drive a tack into the butt of each shake and stretch string between the tacks. Align the butts of the intervening shakes on the string.

To ensure that your courses remain straight, for every three or four courses, measure up from the butts of the shakes at each end of the roof and snap a chalk line to place the butts on for the next course.

Shakes must be cut in order to fit properly around vents, along the rake, in valleys, and beside flashing. Shakes should be cut with a circular saw for straight lines or with a saber saw for curves.

Sheathing

Shakes are normally laid over spaced 1 by 4s or 1 by 6s, which are referred to as spaced sheathing (see page 32). However, because the shakes' irregularities allow air to circulate under them—essential for wood roofs—shakes can also be laid over solid sheathing, such as plywood, or over existing composition roofs. Solid sheathing should be used in areas that are prone to wind-driven snow.

The 1 by 4s for spaced sheathing should be spaced on center the same distance as the shake exposure. If you are going to have a 7½-inch exposure, nail the first board along the ends of the rafters to support the first-course butt ends. The second and all succeeding sheathing boards are then centered 7½ inches up from the rafter ends.

To speed up this process, nail on the first two courses of spaced sheathing, measure the gap between them, cut some

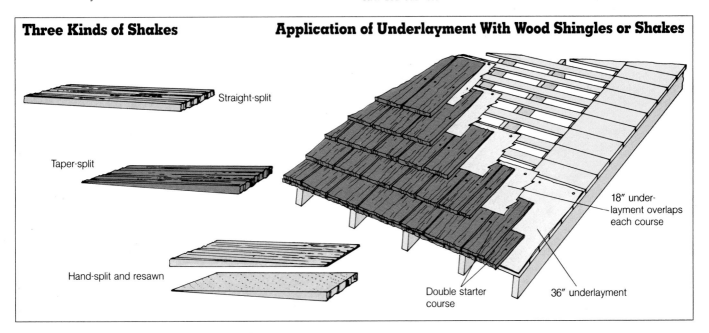

Three Kinds of Shakes

Straight-split

Taper-split

Hand-split and resawn

Application of Underlayment With Wood Shingles or Shakes

18" underlayment overlaps each course

36" underlayment

Double starter course

Wood Shingle and Shake Nailing Pattern

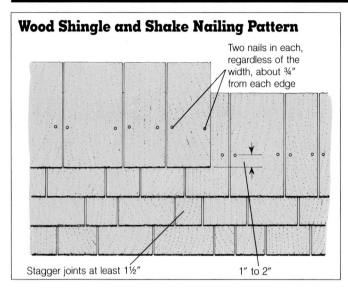

Two nails in each, regardless of the width, about ¾" from each edge

Stagger joints at least 1½"

1" to 2"

chocks that width, and use them as spacers for nailing the rest instead of measuring for each sheathing board.

Sheathe the top 18 inches of the roof solidly. This will allow you to adjust the exposure to make the last course come out even at the ridge.

Underlayment

Before applying the underlayment, nail a drip edge along the eaves. After the felt is laid, nail drip edges along the rakes.

Use 30-pound underlayment. The first strip laid along the eaves is 36 inches wide; all others are 18 inches wide. If you can't buy 18-inch-wide felt in your area, cut a full roll in half by cutting round and round it with a circular saw. Use an old blade or a Carborundum blade. Nail the top edges of the felt strips into the sheathing every 6 feet or so. You can either lay all the felt you will be able to cover in one day, which is preferable, or put down a new strip above each shake course.

The first strip of 18-inch felt is laid twice the exposure distance from the butts of the

starter course. Thus, if you are using 24-inch shakes with a 7½-inch exposure, and the butts overhang the eaves 2 inches, then the bottom edge of the first 18-inch strip would be located 13 inches from the edge of the eaves. Right? The bottom edge of each succeeding strip should be laid out 7½ inches higher than the bottom edge of the previous one. Lay the top pieces across the ridge. At the hips weave the strips together in overlapped joints.

Applying The Shakes

The starter course is laid first, with the butt ends overhanging the eaves by about 2 inches. Extend the edges of the shakes over the rakes ¼ to ⅜ inch. Place shakes with a straight, smooth edge along the rakes for a neat and professional appearance.

Slip the top ends of the starter and first course of shakes under the first strip of 18-inch felt, and the top of each succeeding course under the felt above. On a properly applied

Wood-Roofer's Helper

Wood roofs are much more slippery than composition roofs. If you are working on a roof with a slope of 8 in 12 or more, you can use a homemade roofer's seat to keep yourself from sliding off.

Make this box from scrap plywood or 1 by 12 lumber. The base of the box should be cut at the same angle as the roof. An easy way to do this is to place the board against the roof rake, level the top, and draw a line inside the board

along the edge of the rake. The base should be about 20 inches long and the back a full 12 inches high. Make the seat about 12 inches wide. Cover the bottom with four strips of plywood or some 1 by 4s. First drive six roofing nails through each board, then nail them to the box with nails pointing out. When you turn the box over on the roof and sit on it, the nails will bite in and prevent the box from slipping.

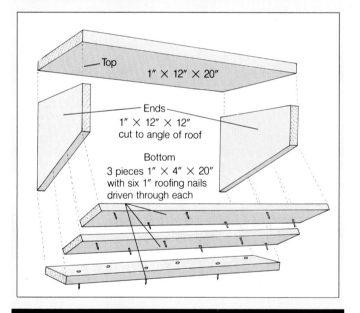

Top
1" × 12" × 20"

Ends
1" × 12" × 12"
cut to angle of roof

Bottom
3 pieces 1" × 4" × 20"
with six 1" roofing nails
driven through each

roof, you should see only felt from underneath and no shakes.

Space the shakes ½ inch apart to allow for expansion. Use 7d galvanized nails placed 1 inch from each side and 2 inches under the succeeding course. The nails should be long enough to penetrate at least ½ inch. If a shake splits consider it two shakes and put a nail on each side of the split.

Use your hatchet as an exposure guide by marking the

handle 7½ inches or 5½ inches down from the top. The joint between two shakes in one course should never be closer than 1½ inches to a joint below or above it. In addition, no joint between two shakes should be directly above another joint in the two courses below.

As you approach the ridge, lay out three or four courses temporarily and adjust them slightly so that the final course exposure will be comparable to the others. When you nail the final two courses at the ridge, the ends will extend above the ridge. Snap a chalk line flush with the ridge and cut all of the shakes at once with a circular saw.

Check to be sure that your work is straight by measuring, every three or four courses, the distance from the eaves to the shakes at both ends of the roof. Snap a chalk line to straighten out the next course.

Valleys

Use 20-inch-wide W-metal flashing in the valleys. To keep shakes along the valleys straight, use a 1 by 4 as a guide. Place the board in the valley, one side flush against the dividing ridge in the middle. This will provide an ample 3½-inch space for runoff on both sides of the valley.

Shakes on the left side of the valley have to be cut individually as you arrive at the end of each course. Lay the last shake at the valley over the 1 by 4, score a line across the shake, and cut.

Because the right side of the valley is a starting point for courses, it goes much faster. Position the 1 by 4 and lay out the bottom shake. Mark and cut, then use it as a pattern to cut all the other shakes, several at a time. Select broad shakes for this.

Hips and Ridges

These shakes are factory prepared with mitered edges. Note from the illustration how they are applied, alternating the direction of the miter joints. Hip and ridge shakes are applied with nails long enough to penetrate the deck at least ½ inch.

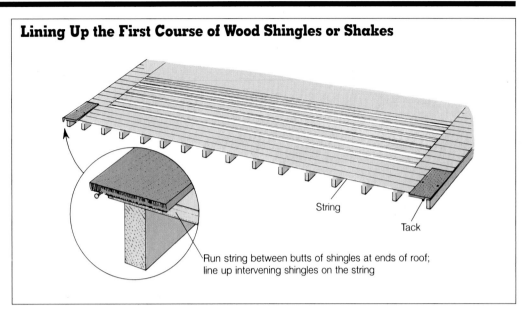

Lining Up the First Course of Wood Shingles or Shakes

String

Tack

Run string between butts of shingles at ends of roof; line up intervening shingles on the string

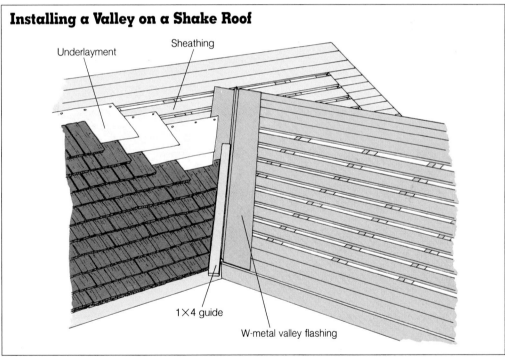

Installing a Valley on a Shake Roof

Underlayment

Sheathing

1×4 guide

W-metal valley flashing

As with shakes next to valleys, shakes running up the left side of a hip must be cut individually as you reach the hip. Use a straight board running up the hip to mark each shake. On the right side, cut the bottom shake at the proper angle and use it as a pattern to cut all the others.

When applying the miter-edged hip shakes, snap a chalk line between the bottom hip shake and one placed temporarily at the top to guide your work. Apply a double hip shake at the eave. For a smooth fit, cut the starter hip shake even with the butts of the second course as illustrated. Apply the first hip shake over that and continue up the hip. Use 10d galvanized nails on hips.

At the top, trim the inner edges of the hip shakes where they meet each other and trim the tops flush with the ridge.

Vents

When applying shakes around vents, carry the course to the vent pipe, then use a keyhole saw or saber saw to notch the edges for a close fit on each side. Slip the flashing over the pipe, then cut two layers of 30-pound felt to fit over the flashing and extend out a foot on each side, as shown. The course above the vent can be notched at the butt if it is too close; if it is too far away, one shake can be dropped down a few inches out of line to frame the vent. The shake should be about 1 inch from the vent pipe. Use a broad shake here.

Next to a vertical wall, as along a dormer, use step flashing as described on page 39.

Applying Hip Shakes

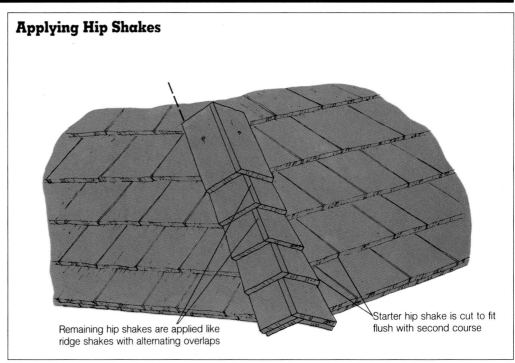

Remaining hip shakes are applied like ridge shakes with alternating overlaps

Starter hip shake is cut to fit flush with second course

Applying Shakes Around Vents

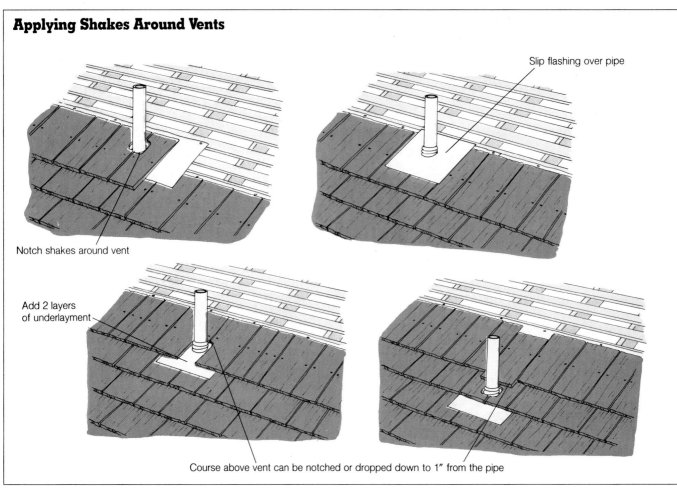

Notch shakes around vent

Slip flashing over pipe

Add 2 layers of underlayment

Course above vent can be notched or dropped down to 1″ from the pipe

INSTALLING A WOOD SHINGLE ROOF

Shingles are generally made from western red cedar. They come in lengths of 16 inches, 18 inches, and 24 inches, and are graded 1, 2, or 3. Only grade 1 is free of knots and sapwood (the outer soft wood of a tree).

Some General Guidelines

In many respects, applying shingles is the same as applying shakes, so refer to the preceding section as well as these directions.

Like shakes, shingles must be applied close enough together to provide triple coverage for a long-lasting roof. Use the following table as an exposure guide.

Slope	16"	18"	24"
3 in 12, 4 in 12	3¾"	4¼"	5¾"
more than 4 in 12	5"	5½"	7½"

Do not apply shingles to roofs with less than a 3 in 12 slope.

Use 3d galvanized nails on 16-inch and 18-inch shingles; use 4d nails on 24-inch shingles. Always apply two nails per shingle, within ¾ inch of each side and 2 inches above the butt line of the succeeding course. It is important to have the sheathing spaced properly so that you won't have to nail higher to hit the boards.

Sheathing

Shingles, because they are resawn and thus lie flat, need good ventilation. They are most commonly laid over spaced sheathing, although solid sheathing is sometimes used for structural purposes.

Sheathing should be spaced center to center, the same as the shingle exposure. Place the first sheathing board with the bottom edge flush with the rafter ends. From there, measure up the exposure distance and center a sheathing board there. Measure the gap between boards, cut some spacers, and complete the sheathing.

Sheathe the final 18 inches solidly so that the last few courses can be adjusted slightly to come out even.

Drip edges are not used with wood shingles.

Wood shingles are always nailed down with only two nails, regardless of how wide the shingles may be. Place the nails about ¾ inch from the edges and 1 to 2 inches above the exposure (the distance from the butt of the shingle to the butt of the shingle above). The exposure, also called weather, varies, depending on what type of shingle you are using and the slope of your roof (see table). Set the exposure with the help of the gauge on the roofer's hatchet. Always check the weather at both ends of the shingle to keep your courses straight. Always nail in the same direction—from left to right if you're right-handed, right to left if you're left-handed. If you see that a shingle is crooked, don't try to realign it after two nails are in it. It will only buckle or split. Remove the nails and reposition the shingle.

It is important that the first course of shingles be straight. To align, let the first one overhang the roof by ¼ to ⅜ inch and nail it down. Place another shingle the same way at the

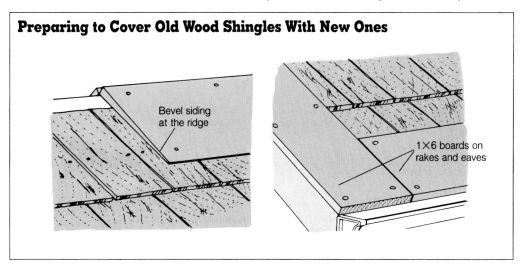

Preparing to Cover Old Wood Shingles With New Ones

Bevel siding at the ridge

1×6 boards on rakes and eaves

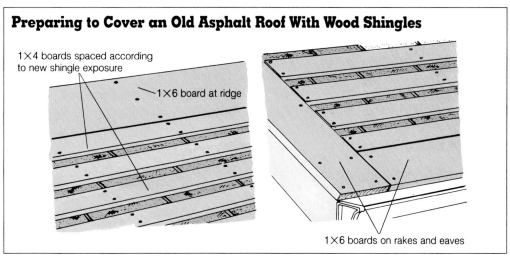

Preparing to Cover an Old Asphalt Roof With Wood Shingles

1×4 boards spaced according to new shingle exposure

1×6 board at ridge

1×6 boards on rakes and eaves

other end of the roof. Drive a tack into the butt of each shingle and stretch string between them. Align the butts of the intervening shingles along the string.

Check for straightness every three or four courses by measuring up from the butts of the shingles at each end of the roof and snapping a chalk line to place the butts on for the next course. Shingles must be cut in order to fit properly around vents, along the rake, in valleys, and beside flashing. Wood shingles should be cut with a circular saw for straight lines or with a saber saw for curves.

Applying The Shingles

Lay the starter course along the eaves with butts extending 1 inch over the edge. Let them hang over the rake ¼ to ⅜ inch. Apply the first course over the starters with no joints closer than 1½ inches to a joint below. Leave ⅛- to ¼-inch spaces between shingles to prevent their buckling when wet.

Spend time to ensure that the second course is perfectly straight by snapping a chalk line. Use your hatchet as an exposure guide for succeeding courses and check your alignment every three or four courses.

As you approach the ridge, lay out some shingles in the final courses to see how they will fit. Adjust each one by 1 inch or less to make them come out nearly even. Let the ends extend over the ridge, then snap a chalk line and cut the ends flush with the ridge top.

Valleys, Hips, And Ridges

The shingling process for valleys, hips, and ridges is just as described for shakes on page 53. The one difference is that lengths of kraft paper (used for flashing around windows) should be laid over the hips and ridges before the shingles are applied, as an extra waterproofing precaution.

New Shingling Over Old

Keep in mind that roofs are heavy, and that local codes may permit three layers or may limit you to two. Check before you decide to simply layer over the existing roof.

Covering Wood Shingles

If the old wood shingles on a roof are in reasonably good shape, they can be roofed over with new wood shingles. Even so, some preliminary steps are necessary. First, nail down any curled or warped shingles. If one won't go down, split it, pull out the pieces, and slip a new shingle in to keep the surface even.

Shingles along the eaves, rakes, and ridges should be removed and replaced with a 1 by 6 board. Measure 5½ inches back from the edges of the rakes and eaves, then snap a chalk line as a cutting guide. Set the blade on a circular saw just slightly beyond the shingle depth and cut. Use an old saw

blade or carbide-tipped blade, since you will hit some nails. Follow the same procedure on both sides of the ridge.

Sweep the roof, then nail down the 1 by 6s along the eaves and rakes. At the ridge use a length of bevel siding, with the thin edge on the down side. Apply new flashing in the valleys and along the eaves and rakes.

Once this process is complete, use standard shingling procedures to apply the actual new roof.

Covering Other Roofs

Applying wood shingles over composition shingles, roll roofing, and tar and gravel roofs is quite similar to new shingling. They must be placed on spaced sheathing nailed directly to the existing roof.

For an asphalt roof remove the shingles along the ridge and hips. No removal is necessary with roll roofing or tar and

gravel roofs. Staple lengths of window flashing paper over the gap as extra protection against leaks.

Use tin snips to trim off the edges of the composition shingles where they overhang the rakes and eaves.

Next, nail a 1 by 6 along the rakes, from ridge to eaves. This provides a finished edge when the shingles are in place. Nail 1 by 6s along the eaves and on both sides of the ridge, with the edges of the boards meeting at the ridge. Finally, nail a pair of 1 by 4s down each side of the valleys to provide support for the new valley flashing that must be installed. Place spaced sheathing over the roof, with the 1 by 4s spaced the same as your shingle exposure. See page 32 for detailed instructions.

Before you start shingling lay the valley flashing in place, as described on pages 35 to 37. Now shingle the roof in a standard fashion, as described above.

The neutral colors of the siding and roof on this home allow architectural and landscaping details to take center stage.

INSTALLING A TILE ROOF

For a roof that is ruggedly beautiful, fireproof, and long lasting (50 years or more), consider the tile roof. Although traditional clay tile is expensive and heavy (about 1000 pounds per square), new lightweight tiles can be installed on almost any roof.

Weight and Slope Considerations

Recent innovations have brought down both the price and the weight of tile. It is now widely made in lightweight concrete that weighs less than 700 pounds per square and can be applied on a standard roof built for composition shingles. Concrete tiles come in a variety of colors and patterns that make it possible to complement or match the siding on your house. Roofing supply firms can give you information describing the types of tiles available, including their weight per square and instructions on how to install them. One of the easiest of the new concrete tiles to apply is the flat tile, which is described here.

If in doubt about the weight on your roof, even with the lighter concrete tile, discuss it with your local building inspection department before ordering.

Tile cannot be put on a roof with less than a 3 in 12 slope without risk of rain blowing up under the tiles. On slopes of 3 in 12 and 4 in 12, it is advisable to lay a bead of caulk under the overlapping edges of the tiles to prevent rain-blown leaks.

Reroofing your home with new tile, as with most roofing materials, offers an opportunity to add new roof insulation. Although the tile itself has negligible insulating value, you can install rigid foam insulation over the roof sheathing before installing the roof tiles. Rigid insulation is available in thicknesses ranging from ½ inch to 3½ inches.

Preparing the Roof

Sheath the roof with ½-inch exterior-grade plywood or, for an exposed ceiling, with 2 by 6 tongue-and-groove boards.

In applying underlayment, follow the manufacturer's instructions, which may call for 15- or 30-pound underlayment, or none at all.

Some tiles are nailed to the sheathing; others have lugs to hook over wood battens. For the battens use redwood or pressure-treated 1 by 2s, spacing them according to the exposure required. Consult the manufacturer's recommendations, but 14 inches is a typical exposure.

Metal drip edges should be applied along the eaves under the felt and along the rakes over the felt, in the same manner as for a standard roof (see page 44).

Valleys should be flashed with W-metal flashing at least 25 inches wide laid over 90-pound mineral-surface felt. Hips and ridges should be covered with a double layer of felt that overlaps at least 6 inches on both sides.

All hips and ridges must have a 2 by 2 board down the

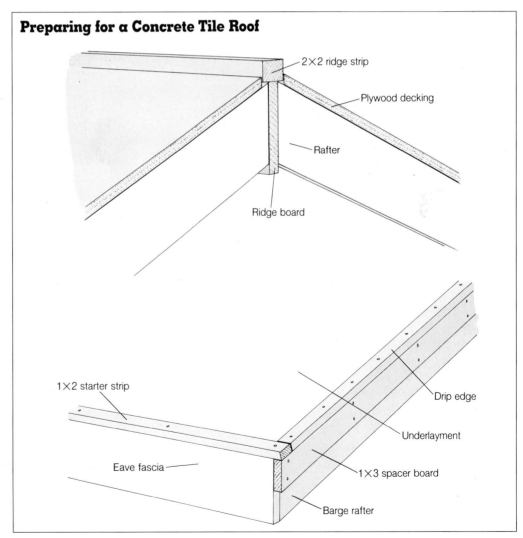

Preparing for a Concrete Tile Roof

2×2 ridge strip
Plywood decking
Rafter
Ridge board
1×2 starter strip
Drip edge
Underlayment
Eave fascia
1×3 spacer board
Barge rafter

Installing the First Course of Tile

Installing Rake Tiles

Installing Tiles on a Steep Roof

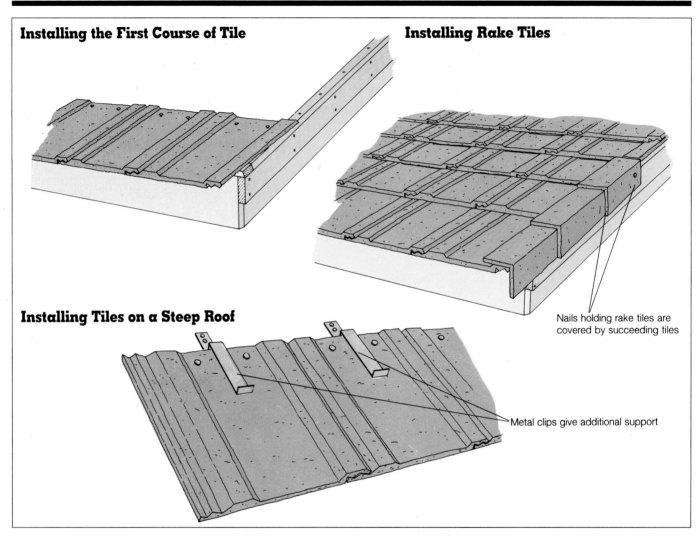

Nails holding rake tiles are covered by succeeding tiles

Metal clips give additional support

center nailed at 12-inch intervals to provide support for the curved hip and ridge tiles. Nail the board to the framing so that the plywood sheathing butts up to it. Also nail a 1 by 3 board along the outside edges of the rake rafters to hold the rake tiles away from the rafters. Finally, nail a 1 by 2 starter board along the edge of the eaves. Since this starter strip can become a dam for water blown under curved tiles, cut drainage notches in the board. For tiles with an irregular profile, such as barrel tiles, manufacturers offer special metal edgings over which the tiles set flush.

Installing the Tiles

Unlike standard shingles, tile does not require a doubled first course. The 1 by 2 starter strip along the eaves serves the same purpose by raising the butt end of the first tile course.

Install the first course so that each tile overhangs the starter strip, beginning at the right-hand rake edge. Nail with HDG common nails long enough to penetrate the roof sheathing ¾ inch. Snap a chalk line to align the top edge of the tiles. Each successive course locks into the previous one.

On roofs with a slope of from 7 in 12 to 10 in 12, use the clips provided with the tiles to attach every fourth row. On roofs with higher slopes, use clips on every tile. These clips are provided by the manufacturer to fit the particular type of tile, and are nailed into the sheathing. Clips are also available for installations in high-wind areas; they hold down the side of each tile, near the bottom, where the clips will be covered by the next interlocking tile.

Valleys, Hips, And Ridges

Hip and valley tiles are laid out and cut in the same manner as wood or composition shingles, using a tile-cutting Carborundum blade in a circular saw. Use a chalk line to mark hips 1½ inches back from the edge of the 2 by 2 center strip, and mark valleys 2 inches back from center on each side. Bring the last tile in each course to the chalk line, lay a straightedge over the shingle in line with the chalk line, then mark

Installing Hip and Ridge Tiles

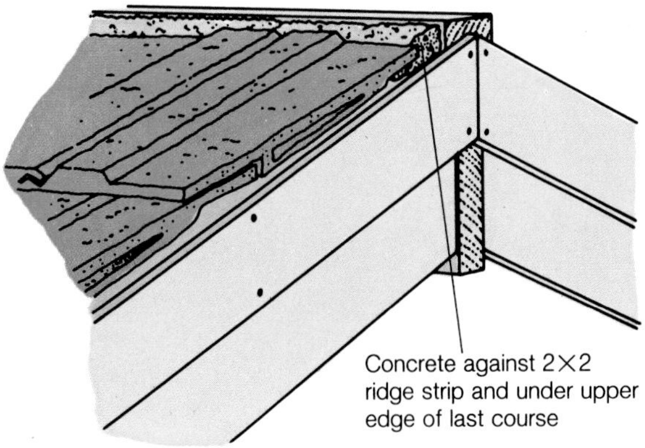

Nail covered with roofing cement

2×2 ridge strip

Concrete

Roof tile

Hip and ridge cap

Concrete against 2×2 ridge strip and under upper edge of last course

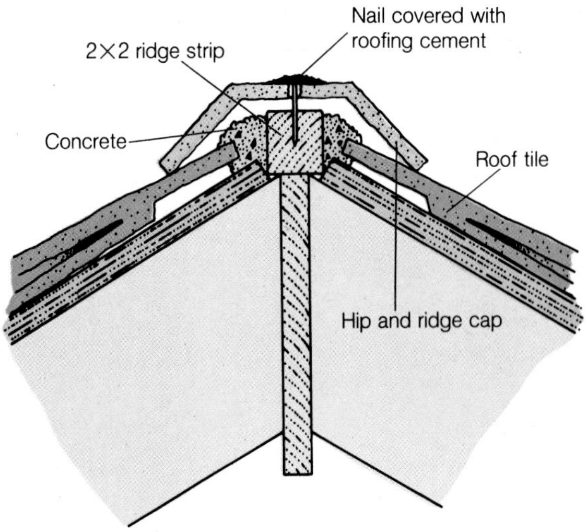

Installing Tiles Around Vents

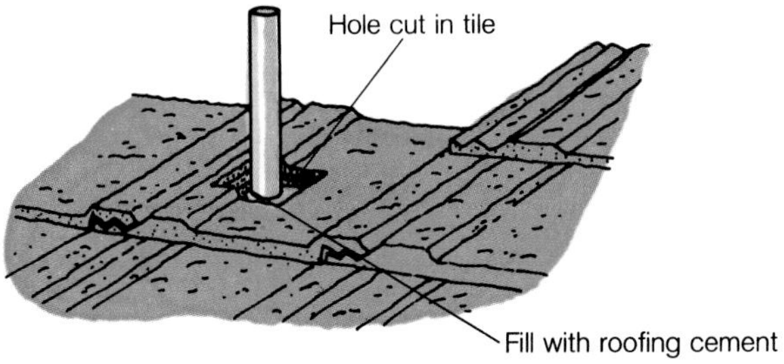

Hole cut in tile

Fill with roofing cement

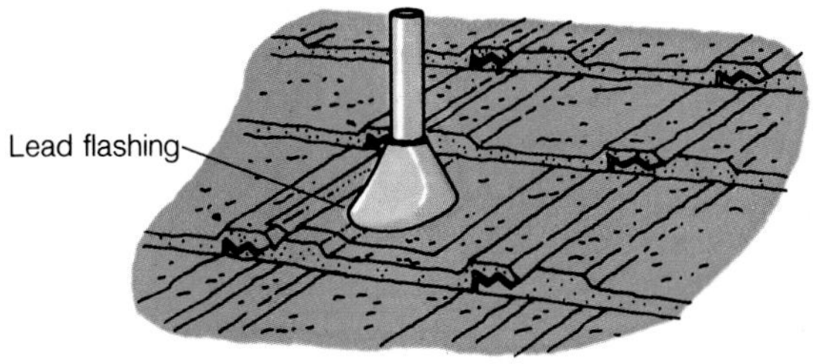

Lead flashing

and cut the tile. Lay a thick bead of caulk under and along the edge of each tile on the valley flashing.

On ridges, carry the final courses to the top, then trim the last course 1½ inches back from the edge of the 2 by 2 center strip.

Both hip and ridge tiles must be placed on a bed of concrete that covers the tile edges on both sides of the center strip. Spread the concrete in place, then nail down the hip and ridge tiles while the concrete is still soft. Cover each nail head with roofing cement.

Cap and Trim Tiles

Cover the rake edges with special tiles or use metal trim provided by the manufacturer. Some of these metal trim pieces are designed so that a fascia board will conceal them along the side.

Cover the hips and ridges with cap tiles. They come in various shapes, either angles or rounded, and should cover at least the top 3 inches of each side. Nail the cap tiles into the hip or ridge cleat, and apply mastic over the nail head and the end of the tile that will be covered by the next cap tile. Start the installation at the

bottom of a hip and at the end of the ridge from which prevailing winds come.

Vents and Chimneys

When a tile reaches a vent opening, it must be cut to fit snugly around the vent pipe. After measuring the distance to the vent and marking the tile, make the cut by raising the blade guard on a circular saw and lowering the moving blade slowly into the tile along the cutting lines. Rap the center piece with a hammer to break it out at the corners where the cut was not complete.

Vent flashing for tile roofs must be specially made from lead at a sheet-metal shop. Apply the flashing in the standard manner described on page 37, then mold the soft lead to the shape of the tile. Fill any gaps between the flashing and the cut piece of tile with roofing cement. The next course of tiles should lap over the top edge of the flashing, just like vent flashing overlaps shingles and shakes.

Around chimneys, install flashing and place tiles as with composition shingles. For details on flashing a chimney, see pages 39 to 41.

INSTALLING A PANEL ROOF

Aluminum panels and corrugated galvanized steel roofing are excellent for farm structures and vacation cabins. Fiberglass panels, factory treated to resist darkening by solar rays, are widely used for greenhouses and patio covers. All are applied in a similar fashion.

Two Styles of Corrugated Panels

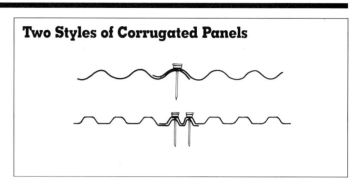

Two Kinds of Ridge Caps

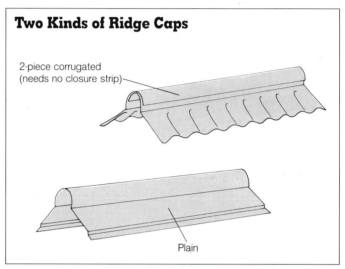

2-piece corrugated (needs no closure strip)

Plain

Some General Guidelines

Flat panels with standing seams, which are widely used for commercial and some residential construction, require professional installation and are not covered here. The lightweight and easy-to-apply aluminum panels readily shed snow, but such a roof can be noisy in hailstorms and rainstorms. Good insulation reduces this problem. The appearance of these roofs can be improved by ordering factory-painted panels. Unfortunately, this nearly doubles the price, which otherwise is comparable to composition shingles. You can paint the roof yourself, but the metal must be cleaned first with muriatic acid. Or you can let the roof weather for one year, then paint it with an exterior-grade metal paint.

Panels, which come in lengths ranging from 8 to 20 feet, are most easily installed on shed or gable roofs. Cutting for hips and valleys will slow down an otherwise fast job. Cut both metal and fiberglass with a Carborundum blade in a circular saw. Be sure to wear safety goggles.

Panel roofing is nailed to 1 by 4 sheathing strips. Space these either 2 feet or 4 feet on center, depending on the roof's steepness and any possible snow load. In heavy-snow country the roof should have a slope of at least 8 in 12, with sheathing strips spaced every 2 feet.

Aluminum panels are nailed down with aluminum nails that have a neoprene washer under the head. Using steel nails on aluminum roofs will trigger a chemical reaction that destroys both metals—thus you must also use steel nails on steel roofs. Nails are always placed on top of a ridge in the panel rather than in a valley, where more water flows. Drive nails so that the washer is seated firmly against the panel but causes no indentation. Panels are normally 26 inches wide, which allows a 1-inch overlap at each side. Put four nails across the panel over each sheathing board.

Steel and fiberglass panels are applied in the same fashion, but the nail holes must be predrilled. Steel is too tough to drive a nail through and fiberglass will shatter without a predrilled hole.

Installing The Panels

If your roof has valleys, install W-metal flashing (see page 35). Drip edges are not necessary.

The first panel should be placed at the bottom left corner of the roof. Allow a 2-inch overhang at the eaves and overhang the rakes by ¼ to ⅜ inch. The first panel must be installed perfectly straight, because all others interlock and there is little room to make an adjustment if it's crooked.

Because the panels come in such a wide variety of lengths, you should be able to install a roof with no leftover pieces. For roofs that require more than one panel from eaves to ridge, order long and short pieces and then overlap them.

The overlap should be 12 to 18 inches, with the longer lap used on lower-sloped roofs, such as those under 4 in 12. For added protection on low-sloped roofs, place a thick bead of caulk under the bottom edge of the overlapping panel.

Ridge caps are factory supplied to match your roof panel configuration. They commonly overlap each other by half a panel width and are simply nailed in place. There are also other factory-supplied pieces, such as rake and corner trim, that you may wish to apply.

A tip: If you miss the sheathing with a nail, lift the nail up slightly, put a thick bead of caulk under the washer, then press the washer in place.

Panel Roofing Assembly

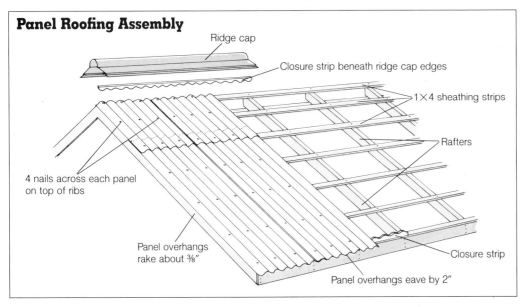

Ridge cap

Closure strip beneath ridge cap edges

1×4 sheathing strips

Rafters

4 nails across each panel on top of ribs

Panel overhangs rake about ⅜"

Closure strip

Panel overhangs eave by 2"

The blue metal roof is a perfect match for the modern styling of this home. The individual panels are crimped together with a standing seam and should require no maintenance.

INSTALLING ROLL ROOFING

Roll roofing comes in a variety of colors and weighs 70 to 90 pounds to the square. It is sold in 36-inch-wide rolls that cover one square. It can be used on roofs down to a 2 in 12 slope with the exposed-nail method, or down to 1 in 12 with the concealed-nail method.

by 6 inches and coat the entire area with roofing cement.

To position the top edge of the first course, snap a chalk line across the roof 35½ inches up from the eaves. Position the roll carefully, then put nails every 2 feet along the top, ¾ inch from the edge. Now nail down the rake and eave edges with nails ¾ inch from the edge, 3 inches apart. If one sheet doesn't reach across the roof, overlap the next piece by 6 inches. Nail down the underneath section first, coat with roofing cement, and nail the overlap in place.

Temperature Concerns

As a rule, because roll roofing can crack in cold weather, it should not be applied when the temperature is below 45° F. If the job must go ahead anyway, store the rolls in a warm area prior to application. If that is not possible either, then carefully unroll them, cut lengths the width of the roof but not more than 18 feet, and let them lie on the roof until they are flat. In very warm weather be careful that your shoes don't gouge the felt.

Apply roll roofing over a smooth plywood deck using a ½-inch overhang along the eaves. Cut it flush with the rake edges and cover it with a metal drip edge.

Exposed-Nail Application

If there are valleys these should be covered first with 18-inch-wide strips of matching roll roofing. Seat it firmly in the valley without bending the center area so sharply that it cracks. Nail one side first with galvanized roofing nails placed ¾ inch from the edge and spaced every 6 inches. Seat the strip in the valley and nail the other side. If you must use more than one strip, lap them

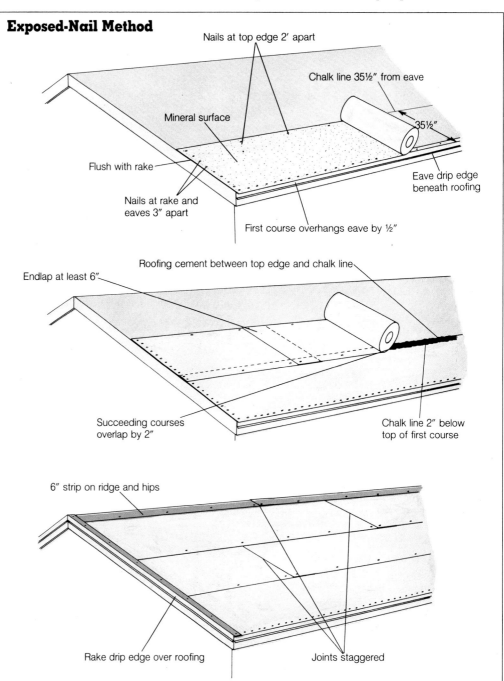

Exposed-Nail Method

Nails at top edge 2' apart

Chalk line 35½" from eave

Mineral surface

35½"

Flush with rake

Eave drip edge beneath roofing

Nails at rake and eaves 3" apart

First course overhangs eave by ½"

Roofing cement between top edge and chalk line

Endlap at least 6"

Succeeding courses overlap by 2"

Chalk line 2" below top of first course

6" strip on ridge and hips

Rake drip edge over roofing

Joints staggered

Concealed-Nail Method

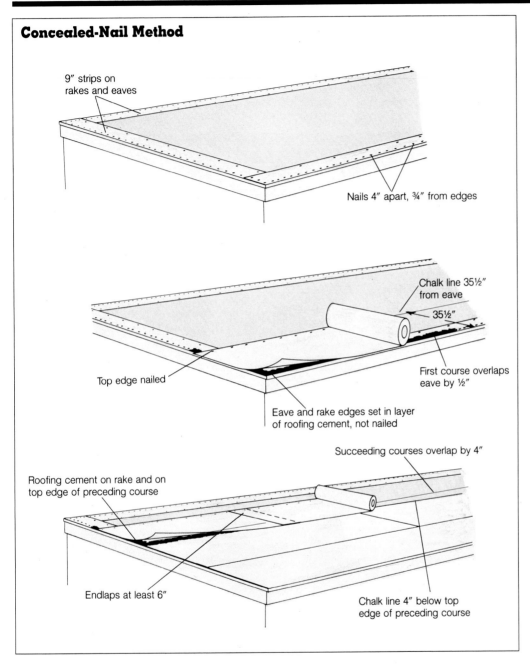

9" strips on rakes and eaves

Nails 4" apart, ¾" from edges

Chalk line 35½" from eave

35½"

Top edge nailed

First course overlaps eave by ½"

Eave and rake edges set in layer of roofing cement, not nailed

Succeeding courses overlap by 4"

Roofing cement on rake and on top edge of preceding course

Endlaps at least 6"

Chalk line 4" below top edge of preceding course

This method is used on slopes of 1 in 12 or less where water runoff is so slow that it could work under exposed nails. Since roofs with such a low slope would not have hips or ridges, in practice this method is used only on shed roofs.

First, install valley flashing as described for the exposed-nail application. Then cut 9-inch-wide strips and place them along the rakes and eave, as shown. Nail ¾ inch from the edges.

Snap a chalk line across the roof 35½ inches from the eave and position the first strip along it. Nail the top edge only, with nails ¾ inch from the edge every 4 inches.

Lift the edges along the rakes and eave and coat with roofing cement, then press the full strip into it. Any endlaps must be 6 inches wide, with the bottom layer nailed and coated with cement and the top strip pressed into it.

Position the second course on a chalk line 4 inches down from the upper edge of the first strip. Nail it every 4 inches. Coat the overlap here and along the rakes with cement and press the strip into place.

Continue up the roof in this manner. When you reach the top edge, cover it and the rakes with metal drip edging. Apply a layer of cement under the drip edges and nail in place every 6 inches.

Snap a chalk line 2 inches down from the top edge of the first strip as a guide for the next strip. Tack the upper edge of the second strip, then spread a 2-inch-wide layer of roofing cement along the upper edge of the first strip and nail the second course over it.

If succeeding courses must be endlapped, stagger the joints so that they are not directly above each other in adjoining courses.

For hips and ridges, cut the roofing so that it meets but does not overlap the joint. Snap a chalk line on each side 5½ inches out from the center of the hip or ridge. Spread a 2-inch-wide layer of roofing cement from each line back toward the center. Cut a strip of roofing 6 inches wide and the length of the hip or ridge, gently bend it in the center to fit over the joint, and nail in place. Any endlaps must be overlapped 6 inches and coated with roofing cement.

S IDINGS

*Choosing new siding should be done with all the care and con-
sideration that you give to your home's interior. Your choice
of siding should take into account your own taste, the style of
your house and prevailing styles in the neighborhood, quality,
cost, and the complexity of the installation process.*

*This chapter covers everything you'll need to know to select
and install the most popular sidings. It includes preparing the
wall, installing jamb extenders, and using a story pole. There
are full instructions for installing horizontal and vertical
board siding, aluminum and vinyl siding, plywood and
hardboard panels, shingles, and stucco.*

*Whichever siding you finally choose, it will not be inexpen-
sive; but you can save 50 percent or more of the overall
cost by doing it yourself. New siding carefully applied will
enhance the appearance and value of your house.*

*The rich texture of the siding, created by mixing several styles of fancy cut
shingles, lends a dignified appearance to this home.*

Siding not only protects the exterior of your house, it says something about your style of living. It's a major investment that you and your neighbors will have to look at for a long time. The siding you choose should be both practical and aesthetically pleasing.

Considerations for Choosing Siding

First, the siding should suit your taste. Do you want the rustic effect of shingles or board-and-batten; the sophisticated simplicity of narrow vertical strips of redwood or cedar; practical stucco; or the clean horizontal lines of traditional shiplap?

The style of your house will dictate some choices in both materials and colors. A stately Georgian seems to call for shiplap; a ranch house may look good in vertical siding or panels, a mission-style home almost demands stucco.

The roof also may suggest a particular siding. One often sees cedar or redwood siding with a shake roof, but going against tradition—say, stucco siding and a shake roof—also can produce pleasing results.

Whatever choice you make should take into consideration the prevailing styles and color combinations in the neighborhood—you don't want your house to stand out in an unneighborly way. In addition, there are several other factors to be considered.

If you plan on installing new siding different from that presently on the house, investigate the various physical properties of each type under consideration to select the one most appropriate for your

needs. Look into the problems of installing the siding and determine what kind of maintenance it will require.

Traditional materials, such as clapboard, wood shingles, shakes, and stucco, have stood the test of time and are still popular choices. Newer materials, such as aluminum, vinyl, and hardboard, are designed to imitate the traditional ones at a lower cost. Although not as elegant in appearance, they can be more economical, convenient to install, and easy to maintain.

Once you've settled on a material, you must select a color, texture, and design. The choices available have never been greater. Manufacturers' brochures and booklets can be a great help in familiarizing you with the available choices. Often filled with color pictures, brochures and booklets also can help you visualize what a particular siding will look like when installed on your home. Cost, appearance, and convenience are all considerations. For most of us, the final choice will involve a tradeoff.

In general, wood shingles and shakes are the most costly materials, followed in descending order by clapboard, aluminum, vinyl, stucco, and finished hardboard. Asbestos shingles and unfinished hardboard are the least expensive.

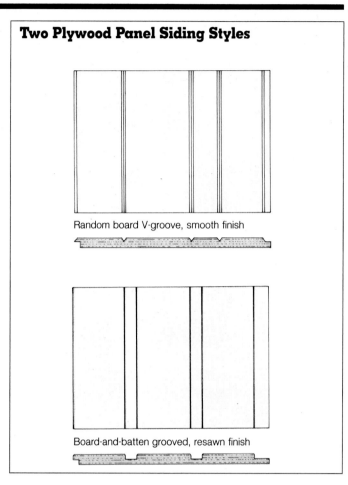

Two Plywood Panel Siding Styles

Random board V-groove, smooth finish

Board-and-batten grooved, resawn finish

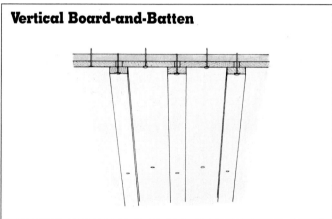

Vertical Board-and-Batten

However, material cost is only one part of the equation.

The cost of labor for professional installation is a larger part of the equation. Although stucco is a fairly inexpensive material, the labor cost for applying it makes it the most expensive type of finish to

have installed. Wood shingles, shakes, and clapboard are generally more expensive to have installed than aluminum or vinyl siding.

To calculate the true cost, you must add in the cost of long-term maintenance. With

Horizontal Board Siding

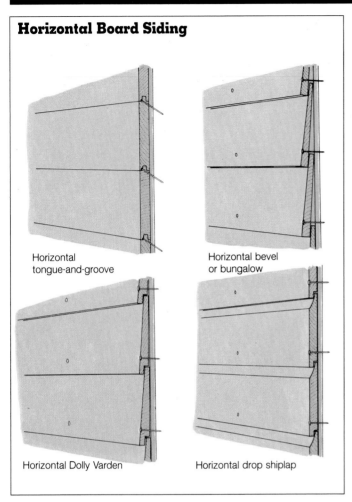

Horizontal
tongue-and-groove

Horizontal bevel
or bungalow

Horizontal Dolly Varden

Horizontal drop shiplap

wood sidings, consider the need for regular painting or staining. Shingles and shakes also will require replacement of missing or damaged pieces. Aluminum and vinyl require little maintenance unless dented or gouged. Stucco is also very durable.

One factor often overlooked by the homeowner is the necessity of a flat, sound surface to which the new siding can be attached. Depending on the type of siding you choose and the condition of the old siding, some preparation of the old wall may be necessary to assure a satisfactory base for the new siding. This may be as simple as installing furring strips to provide a nailable base, or as

complicated and time-consuming as removing the existing siding. If the present siding is in bad condition, or if it's aluminum or vinyl, it will have to come off.

If it is possible to put the new siding directly over the old, you will eliminate a big and dirty removal job, and your house will stay protected while you work at your own pace. But you will also face a problem of having to extend window jambs and adjusting other trim. You still can install insulation if your house does not already have it. Sheets of rigid insulation, called bead board, can be nailed to the existing siding, and the new

siding installed over it. This procedure, in addition to insulating the house, provides a smooth surface for attaching the new siding.

Applying your own siding is a good do-it-yourself project, and you often may save as much as half of the overall cost by not hiring a contractor. Whether or not you should install it yourself depends on four factors.
• Type of material chosen
• Size of the job
• Cost of professional installation
• Amount of time, tools, and skills you have

Even if you are serious about doing the job yourself, you probably should get bids from experienced professionals. The bids will give you a good idea of the installation cost, or how much you stand to save. If you have to rent tools and other equipment to do the job, such rental costs should be deducted from the labor savings. The amount remaining will be the true savings for doing the job yourself, or, to look at it another way, how much you pay yourself for your work.

Overview of Types Of Materials

Choosing the siding for your house is akin to choosing new furniture or a major appliance; it must be durable, attractive, and in your price range. When you combine these prerequisites with the wide array of siding available, making the choice can be difficult. Here is a brief survey of the possibilities.

Wood

In all its varied forms, wood siding still remains a popular

choice for residential siding. It also offers a confusingly broad variety of choices.

Panels

Wood panel sidings are made of plywood or hardboard, which is constructed of heat-processed wood pulp pressed into sheets. Panels are normally 4 by 8, 4 by 9, and 4 by 10. Plywood siding styles include smooth and rough finishes, and grooved panels that imitate board siding. Hardboard siding comes in an even wider variety of styles, ranging from stucco to embossed sheets that resemble shingles.

Panel siding can't really compete with some of the other materials for beauty, but it has the advantage of relative low cost, ease of application, and shear strength. Two experienced workers can cover an average house in a weekend or less. Redwood and cedar panels also are low maintenance—they can be allowed to weather naturally—but other types of wood panels must be stained or painted regularly.

Boards

Solid-wood siding, both horizontal and vertical, runs the gamut of styles, some of them illustrated above.

Shingles and Shakes

Shake or shingle sidings, which give a rustic look, are other top choices in wood. Their relatively high cost is offset by several factors: You can install them alone; they have a lot of visual appeal; they need no painting or staining (although you can do either), and they will last for years. Both are sold

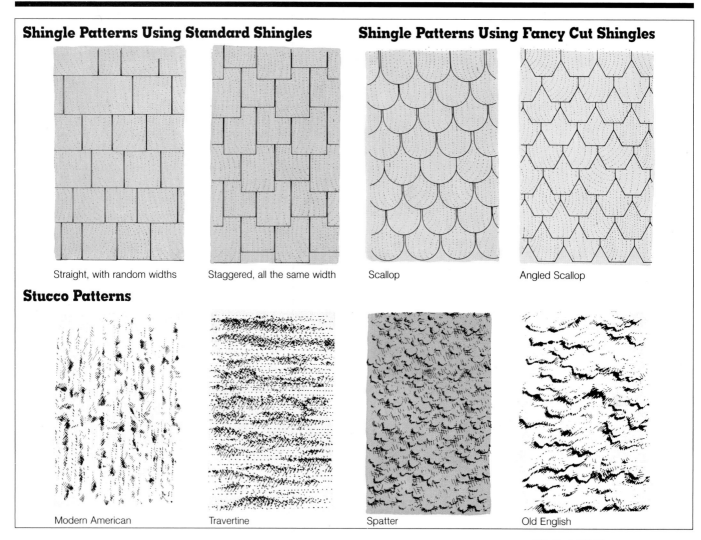

Shingle Patterns Using Standard Shingles

Straight, with random widths

Staggered, all the same width

Shingle Patterns Using Fancy Cut Shingles

Scallop

Angled Scallop

Stucco Patterns

Modern American

Travertine

Spatter

Old English

unfinished or preprimed with paint. They can be obtained pretreated with a fire retardant. They are also available in a panelized format for quick installation.

Vinyl

Improvements in the appearance and performance of vinyl as a siding material have made it increasingly popular. It is available in designs to match virtually all architectural styles. Even historic homes have been clad with vinyl without losing their period look.

Vinyl is applied in much the same way as aluminum and has a similar appearance when completed, although the textures on vinyl panels often are shallower than those on aluminum. Being a plastic, vinyl is more flexible and easier to work with than aluminum (especially during warm weather), but a great amount of precise cutting and fitting is still needed. Vinyl has a high resistance to dents, transmits less wind noise than aluminum, and does not present a problem with chipping—the color is uniform throughout the panel, rather than just on the surface. It can be cleaned easily with soap and water. Some vinyl manufacturers make siding with insulated backing or designed to be applied with drop-in insulation panels. Cracked or broken panels can be easily replaced.

However, vinyl does have its drawbacks. If the sheathing surface has not been properly prepared, unevenness in a wall shows more than with other types of siding. Vinyl can buckle if installed improperly; certain colors are more subject to fading; and it becomes less resistant to impact when subjected to extreme cold. Vinyl also expands and contracts more than other materials, and this must be allowed for during installation.

Metal Sidings

Aluminum siding comes in two basic styles, to give the appearance of either wide or narrow horizontal board siding, and in a choice of many colors of factory-applied enamel. Like vinyl, it can be obtained with insulated backing or to accept drop-in insulation panels.

The chief advantages of aluminum siding are its long life, wide range of colors and textures, and relatively low maintenance. Although fireproof, aluminum itself is a poor insulator, so it often is applied over sheets of rigid insulation, which also provide sound-proofing for those who live in areas of frequent hailstorms. Because aluminum is an electrical conductor, some local codes may require electrical grounding of the siding.

Aluminum siding can be dented easily, which may cause the enamel coating to break, and its finish has poor resistance to scratches. However, individual panels can be replaced. In some climates, the finish may be subject to chalking and fading.

Steel siding continues to grow in popularity as a residential siding. It comes in a range of colors and textures, and resists dents better than aluminum, making it a popular choice in the hail-belt regions of the country. Like aluminum, it is fireproof, but it is not a good choice in areas near salt-water or where there is heavy air pollution. Any breaks or scratches in the surface finish must be touched up properly and promptly, or it will rust. Steel siding is installed in the same manner as aluminum siding, using heavier noncorrosive nails. But steel is much heavier and you may want to have it professionally installed.

Stucco

One of the most durable sidings available for houses, stucco is made of portland cement, lime, building sand, and water. It is applied in three separate coats, with the desired color of pigment mixed into the finish coat, so no painting is required, if done properly. Applying it yourself will cut costs by 50 percent or more but is

recommended only for small projects. It is physically difficult to apply, requires care, and can crack if applied incorrectly or if the house settles unduly. For any major project, hiring a professional is recommended. If contracted out, bids will generally be based on the square yardage to be covered.

Others

There are other types of siding, such as brick, stone, and imitation brick and stone, but this book does not cover their installation, which requires professional skills, experience, and special tools. If one of these sidings catches your fancy, have it installed by a contractor who works with these materials regularly.

Fasteners

Ring or annular-shank nails should be used to install siding. All nails should be corrosion resistant, either stainless steel, HDG, or aluminum.

When installing wood siding, use 1¼-inch or longer box-head nails for shingles and 2-inch or longer nails for shakes. HDG nails are best for wood; they resist rust the best and their rough coating grabs the wood better. If aluminum or stainless steel nails are used, they should be ribbed for better adhesion. Avoid electro-coated nails; if the coating fails, the heads will rust off the nails.

Finishing nails can be used for shingles and shakes if you countersink them and fill over the heads. If the siding is installed over the old wall, the

This period home has been updated with vinyl clapboard siding, which has been cut to fit around the decorative trim.

nails must penetrate the studs by at least 1 inch (1½ inches for plywood and hardboard).

Nails used to install hardboard can be bought with heads that match the color of the hardboard (do not use finishing nails). Combining colored nails with matching caulking compound will save time spent in finishing the job.

Aluminum, galvanized steel, or other corrosion-resistant box-head nails should be used with aluminum or vinyl siding. Nail heads should be a minimum of $5/16$ inch, with $1/8$-inch-diameter shanks. Nails should be long enough to penetrate through the old siding a minimum of ¾ inch. When

installing steel siding use galvanized steel nails to avoid corrosion that can result from the contact of dissimilar metals.

Protective Coatings

Applying the proper exterior finish emphasizes the appearance of your new siding while protecting it from the elements. Metal and vinyl siding comes with a factory-applied finish; wood siding can be stained, painted, or left natural.

Siding manufacturers offer recommendations for the protective coatings best suited for

Blue shutters and other accessories accent the vinyl siding of this home and help retain a traditional look.

their products, and often supply instructions for proper application. Here is some information on the various types of protective coatings used on wood siding products.

Natural Wood Stains

These enhance the natural appearance of wood and often contain both mildew and rot inhibitors with water-repellent additives. Two types of natural wood stains are available: those that form a film on the surface, and those that actually penetrate the wood.

Film-forming stains, such as urethane and varnish, remain on the surface, where they block the release of moisture within the wood, which can result in cracks and blisters. Such stains are not very permanent and require reapplication every year or two.

Penetrating stains are made in three types: transparent, semitransparent, and opaque. Transparent stains protect the wood without hiding its natural color, and slow the gradual process of color change. Semitransparent stains contain a quantity of pigment, which makes them more durable than transparent stains. However, the pigment changes the color of the wood slightly and modifies such characteristics as grain and knots. Opaque stains contain a larger amount of pigment and thus hide the color and grain of the wood, but they have no effect on its surface texture. They do not penetrate the wood as well as transparent or semitransparent stains, and thus act more like paint.

Paints

Available in a wide variety of colors, paints are manufactured with three different types of bases: oil, oil alkyd, and acrylic latex. Oil and oil alkyd paints withstand the elements better than acrylic latex paint, but the latter is more popular because it is easier to apply.

If you intend to paint wood siding, it should be treated with a water-repellent preservative before installation. Be sure to coat the ends of the siding, where moisture is most likely to enter. Once this coating has dried thoroughly, prime the siding. After the siding has been installed, apply two topcoats over the primer. This is especially important on the south and west sides of the house, since they weather the most rapidly.

The natural stains in some woods may bleed through a latex paint. To prevent this, prime the wood either with a stain-blocking latex primer or use an oil-based primer.

Bleaches

For the effect of uniform weathering in a short time, bleaching agents can be used on new wood siding (usually shingles or shakes). Follow up with a water-repellent or transparent penetrating stain after the bleaching agent has achieved the effect you want (generally three to six months later). On some wood surfaces a gray pigmented stain will achieve an effect similar to that of bleaching.

Wood Preservatives

A clear water-repellent sealer will maintain the natural look of red cedar, redwood, and southern red cypress. This has the added advantage of preventing unwanted stains, but it may darken the wood.

ESTIMATING AND ORDERING MATERIALS

Siding materials may be sold by the square foot, board foot, or square. In order to know how much to order (and what your project will cost), you need to determine the surface area of your exterior walls.

Estimating Techniques

To estimate how much siding you'll need to cover your house, first calculate its total surface area. As shown in the illustrations (page 72), the easiest way to do this accurately is to divide the surfaces into rectangles and triangles.

Measure the height and width of each side of the house (minus gables but including windows) and use the formula to determine the area in square feet for each side.

Use the formula on page 72 to calculate the square footage of the gable areas. Formulas for other unusual shapes are given on the same page.

Add all of your calculations together. As a general rule, including the area occupied by windows and doors provides an allowance for waste. Because cutting and fitting around dormers and gables tends to waste material, add 1 foot in height to the original measurements. The total square footage arrived at using this method will provide sufficient siding to cover the house and takes into account the waste factor caused by cutting and fitting.

If you want to be more precise, calculate the total surface area in square feet using the method above, then measure and subtract from your total square footage the square footage of all windows, doors, chimneys, and other areas that will not be covered. Add 10 percent to this figure to arrive at the final square footage requirement. If the house has numerous steep gables or other features that will require much cutting and fitting, you might want to add an additional 15 percent. Remember, it is better to have a little siding left over than to run short. You should plan on having some siding on hand to take care of repairs in the future.

After you have calculated the square footage of your house, also measure the total length around the base of the building to determine the amount of starter strips necessary. Do the same for all windows, doors, soffits, corner posts, and other trim. Add the trim measurements together to obtain the linear feet required, since such materials are sold by the running, or linear, foot. Add about 10 percent to the total to accommodate waste in cutting and fitting.

How Siding Materials are Sold

Siding materials are sold by the square foot, linear foot, or board foot, depending on the type you are buying. Some also are sold by the square, the same as roofing materials (a square will cover 100 square feet including overlap).

Shingles and shakes are sold by the square. A square of shingles contains four bundles; a square of shakes contains five. How many bundles you will need depends upon the exposure (see page 91) used when you install the material.

Wood board sidings are generally sold by the linear foot, or board foot. Convert your square footage into linear, or board, feet to determine the amount needed. If overlap is required in the style you choose, don't forget to take it into consideration.

Plywood and hardboard sheets and panels are sold in sizes that correspond with square footage (4 by 8, 4 by 10, and so on), and the number of sheets required can be determined easily. If the style you select has an overlap, also include enough extra to handle the need.

Aluminum, vinyl, and steel siding are generally sold by the carton. Each carton contains enough material to cover 200 square feet. Trim pieces, however, are sold by the linear foot.

Delivery And Storage

You can either pick up your siding yourself or have it delivered to your house by the supplier. If delivery is arranged, try to have your house prepared for installation when the truck arrives. Even so, you will have to temporarily store the siding, but the less time you have to store it, the better.

Like roofing materials, siding should be stored carefully. This is particularly true of wood materials, which can be damaged easily by rain and other moisture. If you have an indoor location, such as a garage, where the siding can be stored, place lengths of 2 by 4 on the floor and stack the siding carefully to avoid any form of damage. Make sure to distribute the weight evenly; if necessary, separate the layers with short lengths of 2 by 4s or other boards.

When siding must be stored outside, prepare a base of planks or 2 by 4s to hold the material. The planks or 2 by 4s should rest on a foundation of bricks or concrete blocks to keep the siding from contact with the ground and to allow air to circulate underneath. If you have enough sawhorses and sufficient planking or 2 by 4s available, these also can be used to provide a base for storing the siding. Regardless of the base used, the materials should be well covered with a tarp or polyethylene sheeting securely fastened, tacked, or weighted to keep out moisture and prevent the wind from blowing it off.

Although inclement weather will not damage aluminum or vinyl siding, careless handling can. Leave this type of siding in its cartons until you are ready to install it. This will prevent denting, scratching, and other damage. The cartons, however, should be stored off the ground. If they become wet, handling the cartons without spilling the contents can be difficult.

Calculating Surface Area

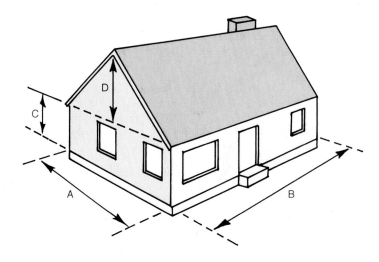

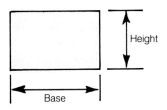

Rectangles: Base × Height = Area

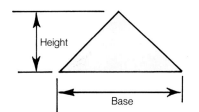

Triangles: Base x ½ Height = Area

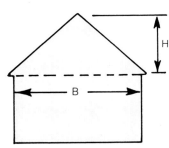

Figure the gable
end as a triangle

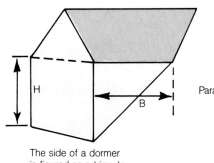

The side of a dormer
is figured as a triangle

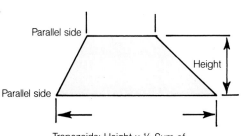

Parallel side

Parallel side

Height

Trapezoids: Height x ½ Sum of
Parallel Sides = Area

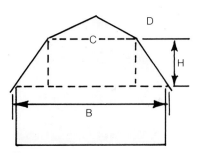

For a gambrel roof gable,
use the formula ½ (BTC) × H
and add for the peak (C × ½ D)

Your preparation will vary depending on whether you are installing siding on new construction or over existing siding. New construction will require sheathing. Existing siding may force you to install jamb extenders. All siding applications will depend on careful leveling.

Installing Sheathing

Sheathing is usually required only on new construction. Whether or not sheathing must be installed over existing siding depends on the condition of the siding. It also may depend on your local building code and the type of siding you are installing.

Sheathing is used primarily to provide a solid base for the installation of new siding and to add rigidity to the walls for earthquake or wind resistance. It also provides a stable nailing surface for siding materials. In addition, some sheathing increases the insulation of the walls. If the existing siding is in good condition it will serve the same purpose as sheathing.

Plywood, the most common sheathing material used, can be applied in large panels. This generally provides enough strength to minimize the need for bracing to prevent lateral shifting. However, fiberboard or gypsum board designed for exterior use can serve as sheathing, as can structural waferboard and ordinary boards.

To sheath the walls with plywood, use CDX or the equivalent with corrosion-resistant nails. Install the sheets horizontally to increase rigidity, and leave about ⅛ inch between sheets to allow for expansion. Nail the sheets directly to the studs, spacing nails 6 to 12 inches apart or according to local code. Use nails long enough to penetrate a minimum of 1 inch into the studs. Overlap the house foundation by at least 1 inch, but do not overlap the plywood sheets at the corners; caulk the seam.

If the old siding has been removed, you can sheath behind window casings and door frames by sliding the plywood sheet into the space occupied by the old siding. If the old siding has been left on the wall, carefully pry off the window and door trim and then reinstall it over the sheathing, after adding jamb extenders.

Some types of vinyl, aluminum, hardboard, and steel siding are designed to accommodate a drop-in backer board, which serves as sheathing and offers some insulation. However, since the R value of the backer board is small, and the material can distort the siding during changes in temperature, you might want to consider the use of a finely perforated insulating sheeting or house wrapping. This has the advantage of reducing heat gain without holding moisture.

If backer board is used, make sure that the bottom of the board rests on the top of the nail rail of the previous course; do not force it down into the butt of the siding panel. The top of the backer board should match the top of the siding panel to ensure that the fasteners penetrate the backer board properly.

Your local code may require the installation of building paper—either felt or kraft paper. Building paper is impregnated with asphalt to make it water resistant; it is meant for installation between the sheathing and siding. It prevents the entry of moisture through cracks in the siding.

Building paper is sold in rolls about 3 feet wide and can be cut with a utility knife. Install the paper in long, horizontal strips from the bottom, overlapping each 2 to 4 inches on the previous strip. Vertical joints between strips should be lapped about 6 inches.

You can nail or staple the strips, using just enough fasteners to hold the paper flat and in place. One nail or staple every 12 inches along the top of each strip will do the job. Once the

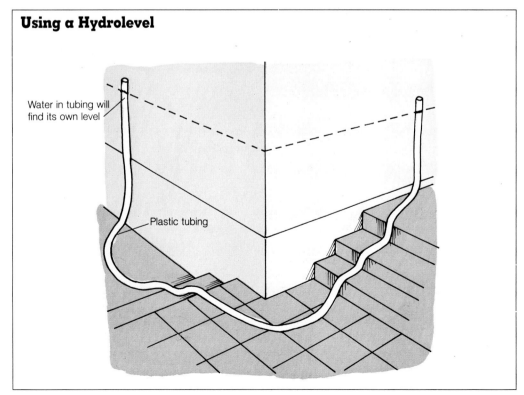

Using a Hydrolevel

Water in tubing will find its own level

Plastic tubing

siding is installed, the siding nails will hold the paper in place. Even if you don't install building paper on the entire wall, it's a good idea to use strips around the windows and doors to reduce drafts in windy or wet climates.

Leveling And Measuring Tools

Most of us assume that the house we live in has square sides, or at least that the roofline is parallel to the bottom edge of the walls. In many cases, however, the house is out of square. It is always better to measure than to proceed on an assumption. Installing siding panels perfectly horizontal when the building is tilted will accentuate the slant of the windows and doors and magnify the problem visually. However, if the siding is installed to follow the tilt of the building, the final result will appear level and correct.

For this reason you need to establish straight lines at various times when installing siding. The most common device is a chalk line, which can be used to mark either a horizontal or a vertical line. Another popular choice is the plumb bob, used to establish true vertical reference lines. You can buy a chalk line with a case shaped for use as a plumb bob, combining both tools in one.

To use a chalk line, temporarily install a nail at each end of the wall at the height where you want the line. Tie one end of the chalk line to one nail. Pull the line taut and wrap it around the other nail two or three times. Lift the line about a foot from the surface and let it snap back. The chalk on the line will transfer to the siding, leaving a mark you can follow. When marking a large area, you might snap the line in several places along its length to make a darker mark.

Other leveling devices may prove helpful, especially if your house does not sit level on its foundation, has settled unevenly, or is built on a hillside. A surveyor's transit or a builder's level can be used to establish a straight horizontal line. If you use either one of these devices, however, follow the manufacturer's instructions carefully to make sure that the device is perfectly level in a 360-degree circle, or use a self-leveling model. An incorrectly leveled transit will give you a straight line but not necessarily a level one.

A straightedge with level may prove useful. This is exactly what it sounds like—a long straightedge with a level built into its center. When it is held against a wall and leveled, you can draw a line along the straightedge. Another helpful device is a line level. This is a small (about 3 inches long) level with clips. To use it, string a line between two points and clip the level over the line. By positioning the level at various points on the line, you can determine whether the line is straight.

A hydrolevel is another leveling device that can be useful. There are several types, but the basic tool is a length of clear plastic tubing filled with colored water. By holding the ends of the tubing against two distant points—with a helper— and marking the water levels, you establish two marks that are perfectly level with each other. By keeping one end of the tube in position you can move the other end anywhere, even around corners, and the water will maintain a constant level. Some hydrolevels have a reservoir attached to one end of the tubing so one person can use the tool without a helper. Another type consists of two plastic tubes about 18 inches long for attaching to a common garden hose.

You'll find a good-quality folding rule and one or more steel tapes useful in making measurements. You may need a combination square, a steel square, or a try square. All three do essentially the same thing—allow you to check the squareness of a line to be cut, or mark a right-angle line for cutting. A bevel is an adjustable square used to lay out an angle, test the accuracy of a sloped surface, or transfer an angle from the building to the siding so that your cut will match perfectly.

Installing Jamb Extenders

When new siding is applied over old, the added thickness often means that the window jambs no longer extend beyond the siding. This is corrected by applying jamb extenders around the doors and windows before re-siding.

Jamb extenders are made by ripping jamb stock to the same width as the thickness of the new siding. The stock must be cut accurately and smoothly; use a table saw, a radial arm saw, or a circular saw guided by a cutting jig.

Wood Windows

For either a door or a window, carefully pry off the exterior casing (trim) and set it aside for reuse. Nail the top jamb extender to the edge of the top jamb, then butt the two side extenders against the top piece. Trim the bottoms of the side extenders to match the angle of the sill, then nail in place. Set the nails with a nail set and fill the holes with wood putty.

When window jambs must be extended, often the windowsills must also be extended. If the sill is round nosed, plane it flat. Rip a length of sill extender from stock the same thickness as the existing sill and nail it in place with casing nails. Set the nails and fill the holes with wood putty. Fill any uneven spots in the joint between the extender and sill with wood putty, and sand when dry. Finally, repaint the jamb extenders and sill.

Installing Flashing

Flashing is needed above wood-framed doors and windows to keep moisture out from behind them. Flashing is not necessary with metal-framed windows because they have a nailing flange that acts as flashing. Lightweight sheet aluminum is the most widely used material for this flashing. Premade flashing is available in standard sizes. Position flashing above the door or window with an extra ½ inch protruding over the casing. Tack the upper edge of the flashing to the sheathing or header with roofing or shingle nails.

Bend the ½-inch protrusion down over the casing. It doesn't have to be perfectly flat against the casing unless you think it looks better that way. If it protrudes a little, it becomes a drip edge and keeps some of the water off the casing.

If you will be installing wood shingles as your siding, keep the butts at least ¼ inch away from the flashing so that they will not soak up any collected water.

When the flashing is on, put the casing back in place as before. Set the nails, cover with wood putty, and paint.

Metal Windows

Since jamb extenders obviously cannot be nailed to metal windows, the windows must first be removed. First remove the exterior window casing. Metal windows are held in place with nails driven through flanges around the windows. To get at the flanges, you must remove the siding next to the window. The flanges are about 1 inch wide, so measure 1½ inches out from all sides and snap chalk lines. Set the blade on your circular saw ⅛ inch deeper than the thickness of the siding and cut along the lines. Save the cutoff pieces of siding. Use a straight claw hammer to remove the nails in the flange, then remove the window.

Now nail the cutoff pieces of siding back in place around the rough opening (you may need to predrill holes to avoid splitting the siding). Place the window in the opening, check that it is level, and nail it in place through the nailing flanges. The new siding will be brought to the metal edge of the window and over the

flange, and then the casing will be put back to cover the gap between the new siding and the window.

The Story Pole

This device is used with shingle and horizontal board siding to keep courses straight and level, and to adjust the siding exposure widths so that there is a minimum amount of cutting above and below window openings. The least cutting and fitting occurs when window bottoms are all the same distance from the ground.

The story pole should be a straight 1 by 2 or 1 by 4 that is long enough to reach from a spot 1 inch or more below the existing siding, or below the top of the foundation, to the top of the wall.

To lay out the story pole, place it against the side of the house next to a window. The top must be flush with the top of the wall and the bottom must extend below the sheathing. Mark the story pole at the bottom of the sheathing, the bottom of the windowsill, and the top of the window drip cap.

Lay the pole down. With a pair of wing dividers set at the desired siding exposure, mark off the distance between the windowsill and the drip cap. If it comes out even, you are in luck. If not, adjust the wing dividers until they mark off equal portions. The length of your divisions must be less than the maximum exposure recommended for the siding. Your supplier will provide specifics on exposure, but as a general rule, a clapboard siding board should overlap the one

Metal-Framed Window With Jamb Extenders

Cutout siding pieces nailed back in place

Nail window over cutout siding pieces and put new siding over the window flange

Wood-Framed Window With Jamb Extenders

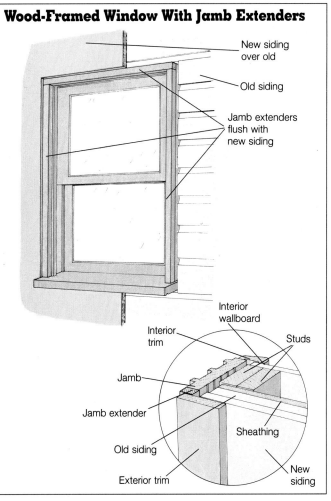

New siding over old

Old siding

Jamb extenders flush with new siding

Interior wallboard

Interior trim

Studs

Jamb

Jamb extender

Sheathing

Old siding

New siding

Exterior trim

below by 1½ inches, and shingles should have an exposure of ½ inch less than half the overall length of the shingle.

By ensuring in advance that the butts of a shingle course, or the top edge of a horizontal siding course, line up with the bottom of the sill and the top of the drip cap, you will make your siding look neater and you will have less trimming to do around the windows.

Once you have established the proper intervals, mark them on the rest of the story pole. Use a square to extend the lines across the pole.

Place the pole at one corner of the wall to be covered and align the bottom mark with the sheathing edge. Transfer the story pole marks to the corner boards or sheathing. Do the same along remaining corners, doors, and windows. As you begin installing siding, use these marks to set up your guide—either a chalk line or a straight board.

Bracing the Wall

The exterior walls of a house must always be braced to prevent lateral shifting. The method you use will depend on the type of siding and local code requirements.

If your siding consists of plywood or hardboard siding, the large panels themselves provide all the lateral bracing required by most building codes. The ⅜- to ⅝-inch plywood sheathing applied over the studs preparatory to putting on stucco siding is also sufficient. But if you are applying horizontal or vertical siding (board, metal, or vinyl), or shingles, you must use addi-

tional bracing. Bracing options include let-in braces and metal strapping. New code requirements in areas prone to hurricanes or earthquakes mandate some kind of structural panels completely covering the studs under the siding. Check your local building codes.

Let-In Braces

You can also strengthen the exterior by using let-in braces, which are 1 by 4s set into the edges of the studs forming the walls. They must always run from the wall's outside top corner to its bottom center. Place the 1 by 4 across the wall from the cap plate to the soleplate at approximately a 45-degree angle and mark the studs where the 1 by 4 crosses them. Cut notches in the studs with a circular saw and finish them with a chisel. Nail the 1 by 4 to the notches and the plates. For more details on installing let-in bracing, see Ortho's book *Basic Carpentry Techniques*.

Metal Straps

These straps are 12 to 16 feet long, with nail holes about 1 inch apart. They are best placed at the corners of the building. They must reach from the cap plate to the soleplate, pulled tight, and must be nailed with 16-penny (16d) nails to every stud they cross. Most importantly, metal bracing straps must always be used in pairs so that they cross at the center of the wall to form an X.

Structural Panels

Materials for structural sheathing bracing must be ⅜-inch or thicker plywood, oriented strand board, or reconstituted

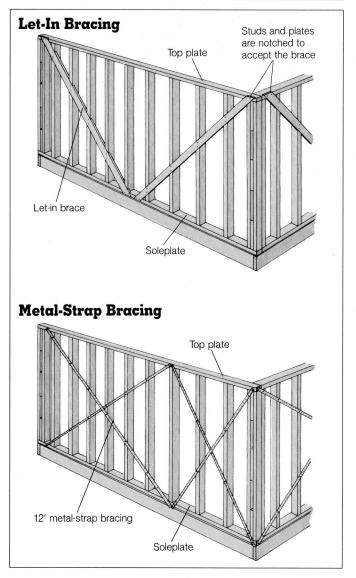

Let-In Bracing

Top plate

Studs and plates are notched to accept the brace

Let-in brace

Soleplate

Metal-Strap Bracing

Top plate

12' metal-strap bracing

Soleplate

wood panels rated at least medium density/structural. These materials should be attached vertically with at least 6d nails or narrow-crown staples at least 1⅝ inches long. Nails or staples should be placed every 6 inches around the perimeter of each panel, every 12 inches on intermediate framing members.

Sheathing panels can be applied horizontally, but this reduces the rigidity and shear strength if the horizontal joints have no blocking behind them. When a horizontal application

is used, some codes require blocking between the studs for close spacing of the fasteners along the horizontal edges.

All panels should be spaced ¼ inch apart at the ends and ¹⁄₁₆ inch on the sides to allow for expansion.

Building Paper

In most cases you will need to cover the wall with building paper before installing siding. The paper should overlap the flashing to about an inch from the door or window casing.

INSTALLING PANEL SIDING

Plywood and hardboard panels are widely used for exterior wallcovering because they are relatively low priced and can be installed quickly. Standard sizes are 4 by 8, 4 by 9, and 4 by 10. The bottom edge of the panel should overlap the foundation wall by at least 2 inches but should not be closer than 8 inches to the ground.

Choosing The Panels

For new installation, panel siding should be not less than ⅜ inch thick; patterned or grooved material usually must be thicker. When re-siding over irregularly surfaced siding, such as shingles or horizontal siding, the thicker and stiffer ½-inch or ⅝-inch siding should be used; over smoother surfaces, such as old panels or board-and-batten (with battens removed), you could use ⅜-inch panels. In areas where high winds or earthquakes are likely, ⅝-inch siding provides more structural support.

Installing The Panels

In new installation, for panels ½ inch thick or less, use 6-penny (6d) galvanized nails. For thicker siding use 8d galvanized nails. In re-siding, use galvanized nails that will penetrate 1½ inches into the studs. Nails must be placed 6 inches apart around the edges and 12 inches apart in the field, or interior, portion. Local codes may require that the corner panels have nails as close as 4 inches on the edges and 8 inches in the field.

Leave a ⅛-inch gap between panels to allow for expansion. When cutting around doors and windows, leave a ¼-inch gap to make the fitting job easier. Gaps around doors and windows should be caulked before trim is applied.

In new construction there is usually no need for felt under the siding. But flashing paper is required around window and door openings, and some builders put a strip of flashing paper down the studs where panels meet. If doors and windows are wood framed, they need flashing (see page 74).

Plywood and hardboard panels must be cut with the exposed face down, because circular saws leave a jagged edge on the upper surface. So all measurements marked on the panels must be transferred in mirror image to their backs. This can be a little confusing at first; double-check your markings and think before you cut.

Panel siding is heavy and awkward to handle, so have a helper on hand. After a panel is positioned, one person can hold it while the other nails it in place.

Panels are normally placed vertically. The leading edge of each panel must fall in the center of a stud. Proper positioning

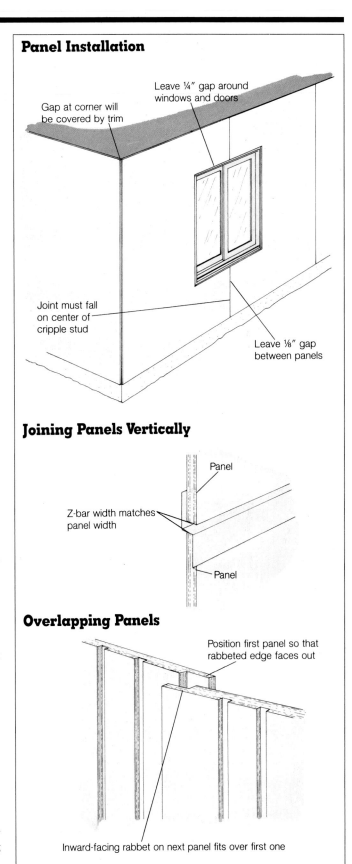

Panel Installation

Gap at corner will be covered by trim

Leave ¼" gap around windows and doors

Joint must fall on center of cripple stud

Leave ⅛" gap between panels

Joining Panels Vertically

Panel

Z-bar width matches panel width

Panel

Overlapping Panels

Position first panel so that rabbeted edge faces out

Inward-facing rabbet on next panel fits over first one

of the first panel is critical, since all successive panels must fit smoothly and vertically against it. If the first one is slightly out of line, succeeding panels will become increasingly out of line. If you have difficulty getting the first one square, spread your corrections over several panels.

For panel styles that overlap, position the first panel so that the rabbeted edge faces out. When the next panel is put in place, the inward-facing rabbet fits over it.

Here's a tip for use in new construction: Apply panel siding before installing rafters, with the tops flush with the top of the cap plate, and then cut the rafters to fit over the siding. This way you avoid having to notch the panels to fit around each rafter.

Cutting Around Openings

When working around openings, use full sheets of plywood rather than trying to make a patchwork of small leftover pieces. No matter how far the panel extends around the opening, the leading edge must always fall in the center of a cripple stud (a partial stud found above the opening and, for a window, also below).

Careful measuring is required here to avoid expensive mistakes. Always leave a ¼-inch gap to make it easier to fit the panel around an opening. Measure from the leading edge of the last panel to ¼ inch from the edge of the opening. Measure from the top of the panel down to the top of the opening, again leaving a ¼-inch clearance. Measure from the top of the opening to the bottom, plus

¼ inch. If the panel fits completely over the opening, measure from one side of the opening to the other side, plus ¼ inch.

Lay out these measurements on the panel with a straightedge, then cut. To make an inside cut, or when cutting an opening in the middle of a panel, use a pocket cut. Do this by positioning the circular saw at one end of the line with the blade over the line. Raise the blade guard on the saw and start the saw. Gently lower the saw into the wood, then cut along the line. With practice, the starting cut will just intersect the right-angle cut line. If you miss, do not back up the saw, because it will likely jam and possibly jerk backward. Instead, finish the cut with a handsaw.

Trim Work

When the panels are in place, caulk the gap between the panels and the window or door jamb, and between panels meeting at the corners.

Outside corners are normally trimmed with two 1 by 4s that overlap, as shown. Some people like to use a 1 by 3 on one side and a 1 by 4 for the overlapping piece of trim for more symmetry. Inside corners can be done in the same manner, or you can nail in a length of cove molding, as shown.

Windows and doors are commonly trimmed with 1 by 4s, as illustrated. Note that the top piece usually overlaps the side trim rather than meeting it at a 45-degree angle, so as to minimize the chance of water running underneath. Caulk the edges of the trim. Flashing

above the trim is not generally used with plywood siding.

Cover the tops of the panels with lengths of 1 by 4 where the panels meet the rafters or frieze blocks.

If siding must be fitted over a water pipe, and the hose bibcock (spigot) cannot be removed, mark the pipe position on the panel and then drill a hole there ¼ inch larger than the pipe diameter. From the bottom of the siding, cut out a strip the same width as the bibcock diameter. Slide the siding in place over the pipe, then glue the strip back into the slot. Caulk the opening around the pipe.

Gable Ends

When paneling the gable ends of a house, first cover the top edge of the plywood across the end of the house with Z-bar

flashing. Order the flashing according to the thickness of your siding. The bottom edge of the flashing laps over the top of the siding and the top edge fits behind the gable end siding.

To calculate the gable end cuts, measure the distance from the top of the plywood at the corner to the bottom of the rafter and subtract for ¼-inch clearance. Measure 4 feet along the end of the house, then measure up from there to the bottom of the rafter, less ¼ inch. Pencil these measurements on a sheet of plywood, then connect the tops of the long and short lines, which will be the line of the roof.

After the gable end siding is up, caulk the gap between the tops of the panels and the rafter and cover the joint with trim boards.

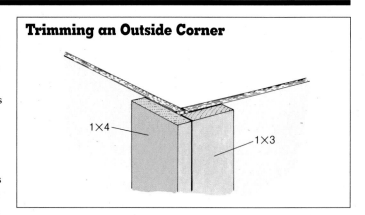

Trimming an Outside Corner

1×4   1×3

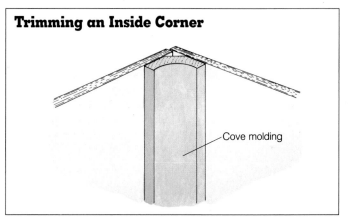

Trimming an Inside Corner

Cove molding

INSTALLING HORIZONTAL BOARD SIDING

Board siding remains a favorite among homeowners. The long, clean lines enhance the appearance of virtually any house. This type of siding may not go up as fast as panel siding, but the individual boards are much easier to handle. Redwood and cedar siding can be allowed to weather naturally; other wood siding must be protected by paint or stain.

house is not insulated and has no vapor barrier, drill ½-inch holes through the siding and sheathing at the top and bottom of each stud cavity. This permits vapor to escape. Nail on 1-inch-thick sheets of rigid insulation; leave ⅛-inch gaps at the corners and top edge for moisture to escape. When re-siding, it is important to locate

all the studs. You may be able to spot them if the old siding has exposed nails. If not, pry off the top piece of horizontal siding, then use your chalk line as a plumb bob and snap a vertical line over the center of each stud.

If doors and windows are wood framed, they need flashing (see page 74).

Choosing The Siding

There are various types of siding patterns available. The interlocking styles are somewhat more expensive than those that simply overlap, but they go up faster and form a tighter seal.

Often, lumberyards and building supply centers don't carry all types of horizontal wood siding, so you may have to look around to find what you want. You should also shop around to compare prices, since they can vary widely. If you are going to cover an entire house, ask the manager for a price reduction. It is often given for a large quantity.

Preparing the Wall

Before applying board siding, install structural sheathing, if needed (see page 73). On new construction, wrap the house with building paper (15-pound felt) stapled in horizontal rows. Start from the bottom and work up, lapping each strip over the one below by 2 inches, and overlapping ends by 4 inches. Carry the felt around door and window openings.

If you are applying new siding over old, you will not need building paper. However, if the

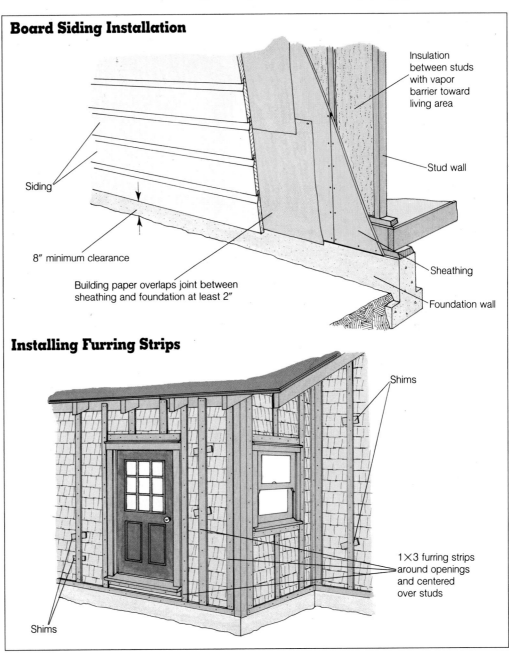

Board Siding Installation

Insulation between studs with vapor barrier toward living area

Stud wall

Siding

8" minimum clearance

Sheathing

Building paper overlaps joint between sheathing and foundation at least 2"

Foundation wall

Installing Furring Strips

Shims

1×3 furring strips around openings and centered over studs

Shims

Detail for Finishing Below the Eaves

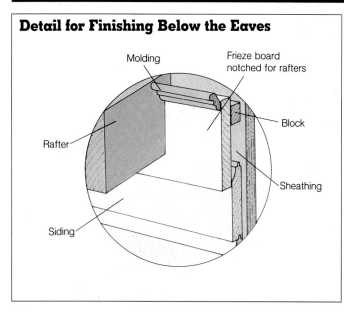

Molding

Frieze board notched for rafters

Rafter

Block

Siding

Sheathing

Detail for Water Table

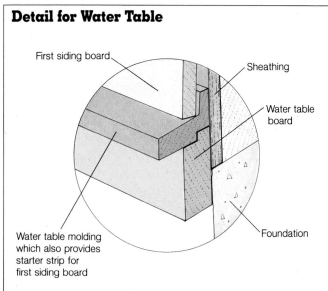

First siding board

Sheathing

Water table board

Water table molding which also provides starter strip for first siding board

Foundation

Sight along the house to spot any bulging boards. Nail them back into place.

Furring Strips

If you are applying horizontal siding over an irregular surface, such as shingles, weathered vertical board siding, or uneven concrete block, you must apply furring strips first to provide a flat nailing surface.

Place 1 by 3 furring strips around all door and window openings, and center them over all studs. If you are putting furring over concrete block, use case-hardened nails.

If the existing siding has trim boards down the corners, place furring strips next to them. Trim boards for the new siding should then be nailed directly over the existing ones. For a closed corner, place furring strips down each corner.

Here's an important tip: After the furring strips are in place, sight down the wall. If you see any inward bowing of the strips where they conform to the inward bowing of the wall, pry them out and slip shingle shims behind them in these areas until the surface is straight. Unevenness is easy enough to correct at this stage, and very difficult later.

Installing The Siding

Put the story pole (see page 75) in place at each corner and transfer the marks to the corner boards. Periodically check your work against the story pole marks to ensure that the siding does not drift up or down.

To check if the bottom of the existing siding is horizontal, place a level on the under edge of the bottom board. If horizontal, use it as a guide in placing the first board. If it isn't, use a line level on a stretched chalk line and snap a line around the house where the top of the first board will be placed.

For clapboard and hardboard, a starter board is needed around the bottom of the house in order to cant the first piece out to match successive rows. The starter board should be about 1½ inches wide and the same thickness as the top of the siding board. A starter board is not needed for beveled or tongue-and-groove siding.

Once the preparations are complete, align the first board and begin nailing on the siding. Siding with formed edges simply fits together. Use the story pole markings to double-check that the courses are straight. For clapboard and hardboard siding, use the story pole to keep each board straight and the exposure even.

When nailing up cedar or redwood siding that will be allowed to weather, do not use steel or even galvanized nails. They will stain the siding with long, unsightly rust streaks.

Instead, use aluminum nails that penetrate at least 1½ inches into the studs. Blind-nail tongue-and-groove up to 6 inches wide, using finishing nails. For beveled and shiplap siding, and tongue-and-groove wider than 6 inches, facenail with siding nails.

Another useful tip for nailing the ends of siding boards, where splits are likely to occur, is to use a small push drill with a bit half the diameter of the nail to predrill the nail holes.

Gable Ends

To cut the boards at an angle matching the roof slope at the gable ends, place a sliding bevel square along the rafter, as shown, then transfer that angle to the board ends.

Instead of carrying the horizontal pattern all the way up the gable, many people do the gable ends in a contrasting pattern, such as vertical board-and-batten.

Blind-Nailing Pattern

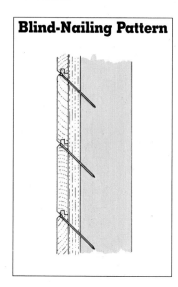

INSTALLING VERTICAL BOARD SIDING

Redwood and cedar are commonly used for vertical siding and are left to weather naturally. Pine and fir can also be used if painted or stained. The boards are usually ¾ inch thick and range in widths from 3½ to 11¼ inches.

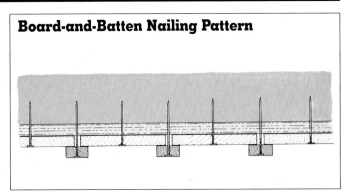

Board-and-Batten Nailing Pattern

Types of Boards

Some styles, such as channel siding, have rabbeted edges for a weathertight fit. Shiplap and tongue-and-groove boards are also used for vertical siding. In another common style, standard boards are nailed up vertically and the joint between each one is covered with a narrow board called a batten. Battens are generally made from 1 by 2, 1 by 3, or 1 by 4 stock; the wider battens are used with wider boards.

Preparing the Wall

When you are applying vertical board siding over exposed studs, as in new construction or when you have torn off the old siding, blocks should be placed between the studs at 24-inch intervals to provide a nailing surface. To keep the blocks straight, snap a chalk line across the edges of the studs. The blocks will also help prevent the studs from warping, which is a common problem with green lumber—wood that hasn't been dried.

In new construction, or where the studs are exposed, the walls must be covered with 15-pound felt. Apply the felt from the bottom up, lap the upper strip 2 inches over the lower one, and lap the ends

4 inches. Cut and staple the felt so that it covers the boards making up the rough door and window openings. Felt is not needed when putting new siding over existing siding.

If doors and windows are wood framed, they need flashing (see page 74).

If the house has no insulation, this is a good opportunity to add it. First, to make sure that moisture from inside the house will not be trapped between the interior and exterior walls, where it might condense, drill a 1-inch hole at the top and bottom of each stud cavity. Then nail on rigid insulation, leaving a ⅛-inch gap at each corner as an additional route for any moisture to escape.

Furring Strips

When covering walls that have an irregular surface, such as uneven concrete block walls or just old walls that are no longer straight, use furring strips to provide a smooth nailing surface for the new siding. Place the 2 by 3 strips around all door and window openings and in horizontal lines about 24 inches apart. Before you start to apply the siding, sight down the strips for any inward bowing. Use shingle shims behind the furring strips to straighten the wall, if necessary.

Installing The Siding

When you are ready to nail up the siding, start at one corner and use a level to check that the first strip or board is perfectly vertical when nailed. Keep it vertical even if the building is out of plumb, because any deviation can be hidden with trim when you finish the siding.

In applying a tongue-and-groove siding, place it with the grooved edge along the corner of the building. Tap succeeding boards into place, fitting a piece of scrap over the edge on which you are tapping, to protect it. Blind-nail boards up to 6 inches wide; facenail those that are wider (see page 80).

For board-and-batten, leave a ¼-inch gap between the boards—they will swell when damp and may buckle. Follow the nailing pattern illustrated above to nail on the boards first, and then add the battens.

Where vertical boards must be endlapped, bevel-cut the ends, as shown, to prevent water infiltration.

Covering Gable Ends

Find the slope of your roof by placing a sliding bevel square along the side of the house and adjusting the bevel to the angle of the rafter. Transfer this to siding that must be cut to fit the gable ends.

Covering gable ends with vertical siding can be done in several different ways. You can carry the siding all the way to the roofline in a continuous sweep, as is commonly done with narrow redwood or cedar strips. Or, depending on the material you are using and the style you want to set, you could put horizontal siding over the gable ends or shingle them.

Corner Treatments

The standard corner treatment for vertical siding is to use overlapping 1 by 4s, or a 1 by 4 overlapping a 1 by 3. Caulk should be applied along the corners of the building before the corner pieces are nailed on.

INSTALLING VINYL SIDING

Vinyl siding has come a long way since its introduction and negative image as a cheap substitute for quality siding. It's now attractive, durable, relatively maintenance-free, and particularly useful for hard-to-reach second floors and eaves. There are even period accessories such as acorn pediments, pilaster sets, and early–twentieth-century porch ceilings.

Choosing The Siding

Vinyl siding is available in thicknesses ranging from 0.038 to 0.055 inch, insulated and noninsulated, for horizontal and vertical installation. Horizontal vinyl siding comes in double 4 inch, single 8 inch, double 5 inch, triple 3 inch, and Dutch lap. Vertical siding comes in double 5 inch, triple 3 inch, and quad 4 inch.

In addition to the panels, you'll need corner posts (inside and/or outside), J-channels, F-channels, undersill finish trim, starter strips, frieze molding, drip cap, and other trim accessories. Read this section to learn where each of these accessories is used, then measure the windows, doors, soffits, and other architectural features that require these special pieces.

Tools and Other Equipment

In addition to the tools necessary for siding installation (hammer, fine-tooth saw, square, chalk line, level, and measuring devices), you will need a radial or circular saw fitted with a fine-tooth blade (12 to 16 teeth per inch) installed in the reverse direction. You'll need safety glasses when

using the saw. You'll also need a worktable, a utility knife, tin snips, a snap-lock punch, a nail hole punch, a scoring tool, and an unlocking tool.

Cutting Vinyl

Installing the blade backwards on the circular or radial arm saw gives a cleaner cut, especially when the weather is cold. Be sure to wear safety glasses and make the cut slowly. Do not try cutting any other material with the reversed direction saw blade.

For some cuts, you'll use tin snips or aviation shears. Avoid closing the blades completely at the end of each stroke. This will produce a cleaner cut. Other cuts are made with a utility knife or scoring tool. Apply medium pressure to the knife to score the vinyl from the face side, then snap it in half. You do not have to cut completely through the vinyl.

Nailing Procedure

Vinyl siding panels contract and expand up to ¼ inch as the temperature changes. It is important that you follow the correct nailing procedure specified by the manufacturer.
• Center the nails in the panel slots, unless otherwise specified,

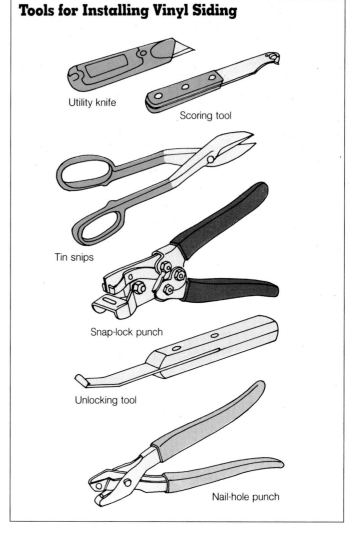

Tools for Installing Vinyl Siding

Utility knife

Scoring tool

Tin snips

Snap-lock punch

Unlocking tool

Nail-hole punch

and do not drive the nails in completely. Leave 1/32 inch between the nail head and panel. This allows the siding panel to expand and contract.
• Drive the nails in straight and level to prevent panel distortion and buckling.
• Space nails no more than 16 inches apart for horizontal siding panels and no more than 12 inches apart for vertical siding panels. When installing accessories, space nails between 6 inches and 12 inches apart.
• Do not nail through the face of the panel. This allows the nail head to show and also causes

the panel to buckle as the temperature changes.
• When installing vertical panels or trim pieces, position the first nail in the top of the uppermost slot to hold the panel in place. All other nails should be centered in the slots.
• When positioning the panels for nailing, make sure that they lock at the bottom, but do not pull them tight as you nail.

The same recommendations must be followed if you're using a pneumatic stapler or nailer. You'll need a special vinyl siding guide attachment to ensure correct installation of the fastener.

Types of Vinyl Siding

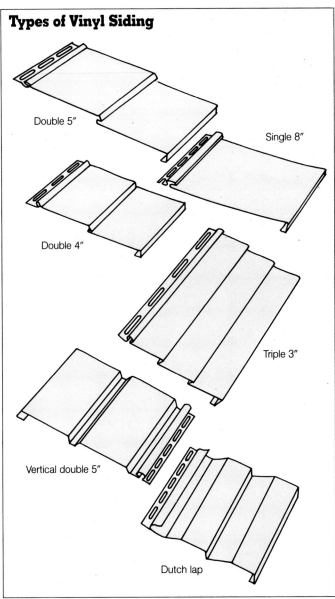

Double 5″

Single 8″

Double 4″

Triple 3″

Vertical double 5″

Dutch lap

Accessories

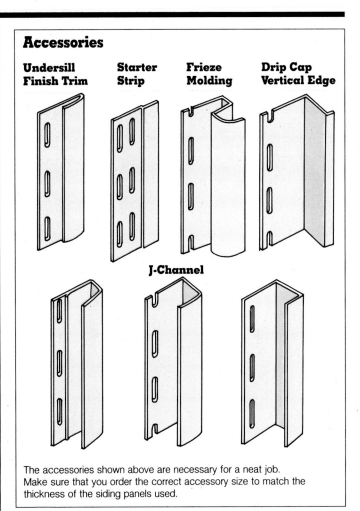

| Undersill Finish Trim | Starter Strip | Frieze Molding | Drip Cap Vertical Edge |

J-Channel

The accessories shown above are necessary for a neat job. Make sure that you order the correct accessory size to match the thickness of the siding panels used.

Centering Nails

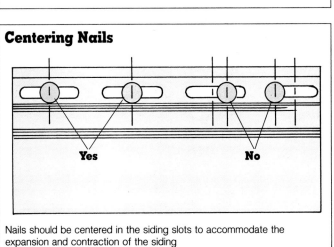

Yes　　**No**

Nails should be centered in the siding slots to accommodate the expansion and contraction of the siding

Proper Nailing

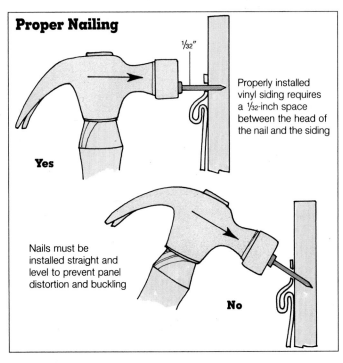

1/32″

Yes

Properly installed vinyl siding requires a 1/32-inch space between the head of the nail and the siding

Nails must be installed straight and level to prevent panel distortion and buckling

No

Installing Horizontal Siding

The first step is to determine the lowest corner of your house, then snap a chalk line at the required height around the base of the walls. The chalk line should be an equal distance from the eaves or windows at each end.

If the lower part of a panel requires cutting for installation over steps, porches, and so on, install furring under the panel to provide rigidity and to establish a correct cant, or angle. Seal the cut edge of the panel by securing undersill trim to the wall.

Install a starter strip along the chalk line, leaving space for corner posts or J-channels. Maintain a minimum of ¼ inch between the ends of the starter strips for expansion. If your siding uses backer boards, fur out the starter strip to the same thickness.

If you plan on installing a vinyl soffit, invert and mount a length of F-channel at the top edge of the siding. Mount a second inverted length of F-channel on the fascia so that the channels are parallel. The two channels are used to hold the soffit panels.

Install corner posts, positioning them ¼ inch below the

Snapping a Chalk Line

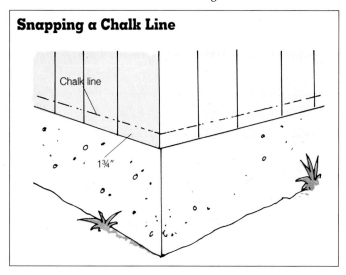

Chalk line

1¾"

Expansion Space

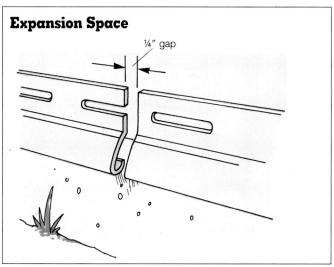

¼" gap

Installing a Corner Post

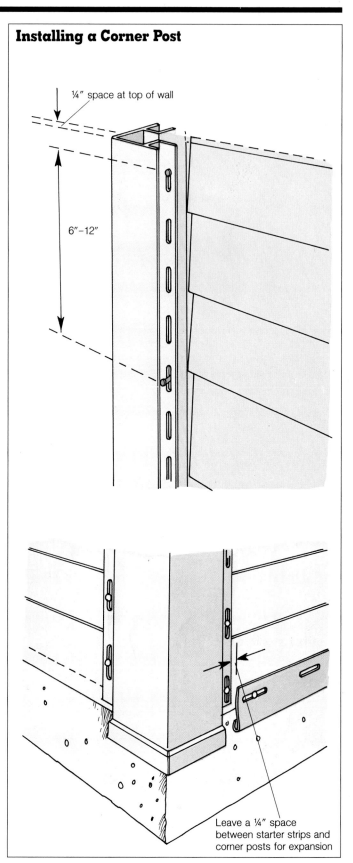

¼" space at top of wall

6"–12"

Leave a ¼" space between starter strips and corner posts for expansion

Installing Window Trim

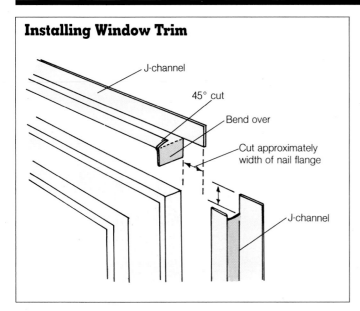

J-channel

45° cut

Bend over

Cut approximately
width of nail flange

J-channel

Inserting Flashing

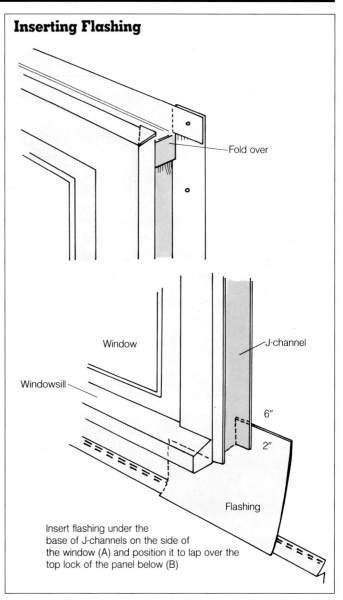

Fold over

Window

Windowsill

J-channel

6"

2"

Flashing

Insert flashing under the
base of J-channels on the side of
the window (A) and position it to lap over the
top lock of the panel below (B)

top trim. Tack each post in place with a nail at the top of the upper slot, then check with a plumb bob to make sure that the post is vertical. Install the nails in the center of their slots at 6-inch or 12-inch intervals.

This will allow the post to expand and contract at the bottom. If the wall height exceeds the length of the corner post, cut a second section to overlap the first by 1 inch. The same technique is used for installing inside and outside corner posts.

Make sure all windows and doors are properly caulked, then install J-channel around each. Cut the side members longer than the height required and notch at the top. Miter-cut the free flange at a 45-degree angle and bend the tab down. This will act as flashing over the side members. Install the sill trim first, the jambs second, and the head last. You may want to install additional flashing to help stop water from seeping behind the siding. If so, cut and slip the flashing under the base of the J-channel, positioning it to lap over the top lock of the panel underneath.

Lock the first panel of siding into the lip of the starter strip, slide it into the corner post (leaving ¼ inch for expansion), and nail at 16-inch intervals. Overlap subsequent panels in the same course 1¼ inches at the prenotched ends, running the laps away from the most common view on each wall, so that the joints will not be seen as easily. The factory-notched end should go under the unnotched end of the next panel. Do not nail closer than 6 inches to any lap joint.

After the starter course has been installed, start the second course, locking each panel into the one under it. Lap factory ends together and stagger the laps at least 24 inches to avoid having the seams too close to each other, unless separated by several courses. Some manufacturers suggest that you cut about 1½ inches of the nailing flange away from the end of one panel when overlapping. If you're using 8-inch noninsulated panels, backer tabs can be inserted behind the joints to add rigidity.

Furring Strip

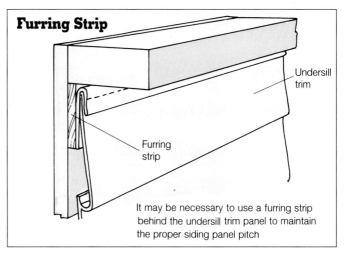

Undersill
trim

Furring
strip

It may be necessary to use a furring strip
behind the undersill trim panel to maintain
the proper siding panel pitch

Fit the siding around the windows and doors and into the corner posts, leaving ¼-inch clearance at all trim areas for expansion. If there is less than a panel width between the top of a panel and a window or other opening, position a panel snugly under the opening and mark cutout dimensions. Use tin snips for vertical cuts; use a utility knife or scoring tool for scoring horizontal cuts, then snap out the section. If panels have an insulation backing, cut the insulation before scoring the panels. To hold the cutout section of panel securely under a window, install a strip of undersill trim beneath the windowsill. You may have to use furring underneath the trim to keep a correct siding slope when the panel is locked into the trim.

Do not nail the top course. Nail a strip of undersill trim just under the soffit track, or along the top course of the old siding. Measure the distance between the top course and the trim strip and cut the panels to fit. Using your snap-lock punch, indent the upper edge of each panel at 6-inch intervals so that the raised ears, or lugs, are on the outer face. Lock the bottom of the panel into the lip of the panel under it and push the top of the panel into the trim strip; the raised ears will catch and hold the panel in the trim strip.

If you need to remove a panel after it has been installed, hook the unlocking tool into the locking strip of the panel above the one you want to remove. Apply a firm downward pressure on the tool and slide it the length of the panel. This will free the panel enough so that you can reach underneath it and remove the nails holding the panel you want to remove.

When you're finished it's a good idea to wash the siding with a mild soap solution to remove fingerprints or other dirt, then rinse with clear water.

Installing Vertical Siding

Snap a level chalk line around the base of the walls at a point 1 inch higher than the lowest corner. Install window head flashing or a drip cap along the chalk line to serve as the vertical base. When joining two lengths of head flashing or drip cap, backtrim the nailing flanges about an inch, then overlap ½ inch to provide a proper joint.

If you plan on installing a vinyl soffit, invert and mount a length of F-channel at the top edge of the siding. Mount a second length on the fascia so that the channels are parallel. The channels will hold the soffit panels. If no soffit is used, install J-channel at the tops of the side walls. At the gable ends, snap a level chalk line along the base of the gable and install J-channel. Lap where needed and be sure to allow for expansion.

Install corner posts, positioning them ¼ inch below the top trim. Tack each post in place with a nail at the top of the upper slot, then check with a plumb bob to make sure that the post is vertical. Install the nails in the center of their slots at 6-inch or 12-inch intervals. This will allow the post to expand and contract at the bottom. The corner posts should extend ¼ to ½ inch below the vertical base. If the wall height exceeds the length of the corner post, cut a second section to overlap the first by 1 inch. The same technique is used for installing both inside and outside corner posts.

Proper Nailing of Vertical Siding

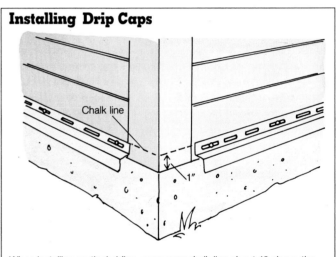

When installing vertical panels or trim, the top nail should go at the top of the slot; all other nails are centered in their slots

Installing Drip Caps

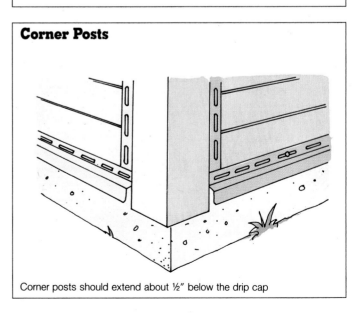

When installing vertical siding, snap your chalk line about 1″ above the foundation. Install the drip caps with sufficient space for the corner post.

Corner Posts

Corner posts should extend about ½″ below the drip cap

Gable End

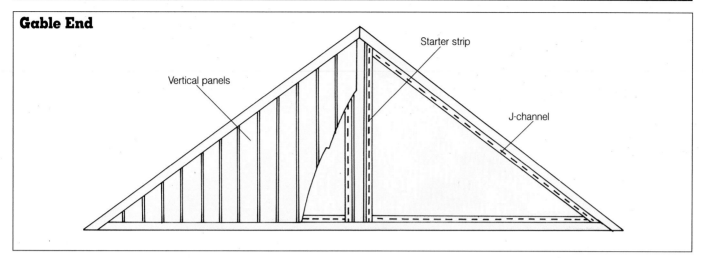

Vertical panels

Starter strip

J-channel

Trim around all windows, doors, and other openings in the same way you would if installing horizontal siding. Now you're ready to begin installing the strips.

Start from the center of the wall and drop a plumb line to mark the location of the starter strip. Position this strip exactly on the plumb marks, leaving a ¼-inch gap at the top and bottom for expansion. Install the first nails in the uppermost end of the top nail slots (use this nailing procedure for all other vertical strips), then nail the rest of the strip at 6-inch or 12-inch intervals.

Cut the remaining panels to fit between the base and trim strips, leaving ¼-inch gaps for expansion. Working from the starter strip, insert each panel into the top strip, lower it onto the bottom strip, and lock to the adjoining panel, nailing at 6- or 12-inch intervals.

If more than one course is necessary because of the height of the house, install head flashing on top of the J-channel and start the second course with a ¼-inch gap at the flashing.

Measure, mark, and cut the panels to fit around windows,

doors, and other openings in the same way you would if installing horizontal siding. When you reach the corner, nail a length of undersill trim inside the corner post and fur it as required to keep it straight. Indent the edge of the panel at 6-inch intervals with the snap-lock punch so that the raised ears, or lugs, are on the outer face. Lock the edge of the panel into the corner strip; the raised ears will catch and hold the panel in the trim strip.

To cover the gable ends, install J-channel along the rake edge of the roof. Run head flashing (vertical base) at the base of the gable on top of the J-channel holding the side wall sections. Use starter strips to split the triangle into two smaller triangles, as shown in the illustration. Cover the gable with vertical panels, cutting each to fit the slant of the roof. Don't forget to allow ¼ inch for expansion at each end.

You can make an accurate pattern for cutting the panels to the roof slant with two 10-inch or longer scraps of siding. Lock one piece onto the starter strip under the eaves. Position the

Trimming Nailing Flanges

1"

Lap ½"

Back-trim the nailing flanges on starter strips about 1" and overlap them ½" for a smooth joint

Using Head Flashing

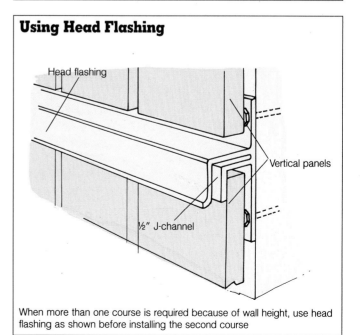

Head flashing

Vertical panels

½" J-channel

When more than one course is required because of wall height, use head flashing as shown before installing the second course

Using Inverted F-channel to Hold a Soffit

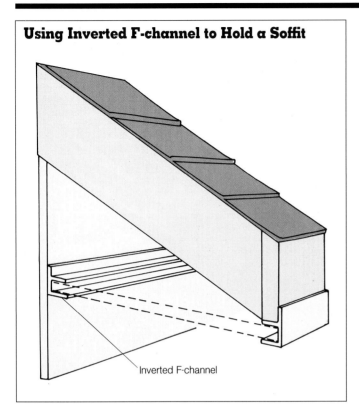

Inverted F-channel

Finishing a Soffit

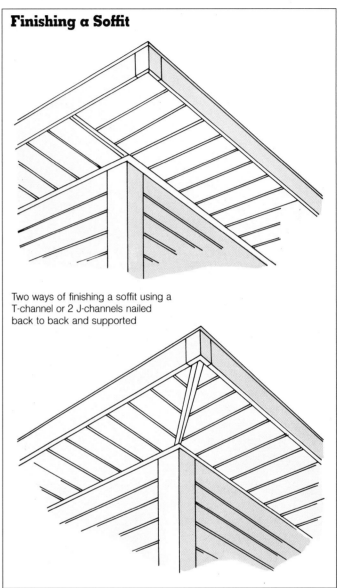

Two ways of finishing a soffit using a T-channel or 2 J-channels nailed back to back and supported

edge of the other piece against and in line with the roofline. Mark and cut the first piece.

This will give you a pattern for all cuts to be made on that side of the gable. Repeat this procedure to make a pattern for the other side of the gable.

Installing a Soffit

Soffit panels differ from regular vinyl panels. They may be solid or have a perforated surface to provide ventilation in the overhang. However, they are installed in the same way; their sides lock into each other and the ends fit into F-channels. One length of inverted F-channel is installed at the top edge of the siding. A second length is installed on the fascia. The soffit panels are cut to fit between the two channels (allowing ¼ inch for expansion), inserted in the channels, and locked together.

Use a channel extension at the corners. This can be a T-channel or a double track made by attaching two J-channels back to back and fastened at the bottom of a 2 by 2 strip nailed between the wall and fascia. It allows one run of soffit panels to fill the corner gap, while the other run ends at the channel extension. If you wish, you can install the channel extension between the corner post and corner of the fascia. However, this will require a considerable amount of cutting to make the final strips fit.

Nail strips of undersill trim at the top of the fascia flush with the roofline. Cut the fascia covers to the required width, then use the snap-lock punch to indent the top edges at 6-inch intervals so that the raised ears, or lugs, are on the outer face. When the fascia covers are hooked over the bottom of the

F-channel and their top edges inserted into the undersill trim, the raised ears will lock the covers into the trim.

To make corner caps for the fascia covers, cut a 6-inch piece and lightly score a vertical centerline on the back. Cut out a 90-degree section of the flange to allow for bending, then make one or two indents on the top with the snap-lock punch. The corner cap can be bent and snapped into place, providing a clean look to the fascia.

Covering Window Trim

Some vinyl manufacturers offer coverings for windowsills and casings that can be installed before the window trim. Their installation differs according to manufacturer and design, but all are fastened either with nails or vinyl cement. If these coverings catch your fancy, follow the installation directions provided by the manufacturer.

INSTALLING ALUMINUM AND HARDBOARD SIDING

Two other man-made materials used to manufacture board siding are aluminum and hardboard. Both come prepainted and ready to install, but installation techniques are somewhat different. Their embossed grain patterns and traditional board profiles give them a strong resemblance to real board siding.

Aluminum Siding

The materials, tools, and methods of cutting and installing aluminum siding are virtually the same as for vinyl siding. The differences are described below.

• Wear safety glasses and heavy gloves when cutting aluminum siding. Cutting creates many small dangerous metal slivers.

• Finishing trim is made from aluminum coil stock, using a tool called a brake to bend the material to the desired angles for corners, windows, and fascias. This tool is available from tool rental companies.

• Use only aluminum.

• Installing a soffit requires only the wall channel. The panels are cut to cover about three quarters of the fascia bottom, leaving room for the fascia cover. Cover caps are nailed to the top of the fascia, where the gutters will conceal the nails.

• When lapping panels on the same course, insert a small metal backer plate or tab behind each joint, nailing it to the wall before securing the panel. This extra support gives greater stability to the panels.

• Corner posts and starter strips are not used with vertical siding. Instead of starting in the center start about a foot from the end of the wall. Trim the simulated batten from the outer edge of the first panel and plumb carefully, then nail on both sides. Continue across the wall, fitting the final panel to extend beyond the corner. Mark the panel at the top and bottom about ⅛ inch beyond the corner, then remove the panel from the wall. Use a brake tool, or secure the panel to your worktable with a board across its surface and clamps at each end. Use a second board to carefully bend the panel overhang to a 90-degree angle at the marks. Place the bent panel on the wall and nail around the corner. When you reach your starting point, install a length of general-purpose trim over the nail heads at the outer edge of the starter panel to accept the last corner panel.

• When using corner caps on 8-inch siding, install the siding ¼ inch (insulated) or ¾ inch (noninsulated) back from the corners. Install outside corner caps once each course of siding on the adjoining side has been installed. Seat the cap in the siding panel interlock and nail through the prepunched holes.

• Use gutter seal adhesive to hold aluminum panels where there is no other means of support. This performs the same function as the indented ears made on vinyl with a snap-lock punch.

Hardboard Board

This siding is available in lap boards as well as sheets or panels (discussed under Panel Siding). The boards are 6 to 12 inches in width, and up to 16 feet in length. Although the boards are easier to handle than the panels, it takes longer to cover the wall area.

Besides low cost, hardboard siding has certain advantages over vinyl or aluminum. Its damage-resistant surface is not easily dented; it comes in a wider variety of finishes and textures than other types of siding, and it is not affected by temperature changes. When preprimed siding is installed, it can be left exposed for 90 days, giving you an opportunity to apply the final coat at your convenience. It also can be bought with a tough, long-lasting finish applied at the factory.

Horizontal or vertical application of hardboard siding is essentially the same as conventional board siding. Only ordinary carpenter's tools are required to cut, fit, and apply the siding. The material can be cut and fastened by conventional methods.

The installation of hardboard siding in progress reveals the width and length of the panels being used.

The remodeling of this classic shingle-style home included re-siding it with new wood shingles. Note the details: how the shingle courses line up with the bottoms of the windows, how the overlapping corner shingles alternate direction with each course, and how the vertical alignment of seams between individual shingles is staggered for at least three courses.

INSTALLING SHINGLE SIDING

Apart from sheer attractiveness, cedar shingles have several advantages over other siding: They are long lasting and require no painting, and you can do the job without help. Although shingles are somewhat more expensive than other types of siding, you will save on maintenance.

Choosing The Shingles

Two types of cedar shingles are commonly used: red cedar, which weathers to a silvery gray, medium brown, or dark brown, depending on local climatic conditions, and white cedar, which weathers to a silvery gray. Both types are sold in grades 1, 2, and 3.

There are also fancy-cut shingles, which allow you to create a variety of patterns in the shingling. They are generally grade 1, and expensive. They are applied in the same manner as standard shingles.

Shingles are sold in lengths of 16 inches, 18 inches, and 24 inches. The maximum exposure should be ½ inch less than half the overall length, which works out to 7½ inches, 8½ inches, and 11½ inches. These exposures can be reduced for better protection and to make courses line up with the story pole layout (see page 75).

Calculating Your Needs

Wood shingles are sold in bundles made up according to the length and number of shingles. To order enough for your house, all you need to know is the square footage of your walls. From this figure your supplier can quickly estimate your needs. You should allow 10 to 15 percent extra for waste. You can return any unused bundles, but you might keep one on hand for later repairs.

Preparing the Wall

Shingling on walls is normally applied over solid sheathing. The corners and all door and window openings should be covered with kraft paper to protect against possible water infiltration. However, over the wall sheathing use red resin paper or other building paper that allows the shingles to breathe while still blocking wind infiltration.

Cut and fit metal flashing over all door and window casings before the shingles are applied (see page 74). The flashing should extend 4 to 6 inches up the wall.

It is advisable to paint all window jambs, sashes, and casings before the shingles go on.

Single vs. Double Coursing

When shingles are installed in single courses, the rows are close together, with the bottom half of one course overlapping the top half of the course below it. As a general rule shingles should have an exposure of ½ inch less than half the overall length of the shingle.

When shingles are double-coursed, each is installed over an undercourse shingle of the same length, using a length of shiplap to establish a uniform overhang. Double coursing allows the rows of shingles to be installed farther apart, with a maximum exposure about 4 inches less than the full length of the shingles.

If you double-course, you must buy twice the number of shingles required by your measurements. However, a lesser quality and inexpensive grade of shingle will serve the purpose for the undercourse, since these shingles will not be seen.

Installing The Shingles

After the wall has been prepared, use the story pole to lay out shingle exposures. The idea is to have shingle butts in line with the bottom of the windowsill and the top of the drip cap, if possible, to minimize cutting shingles to fit.

The first shingle course across the bottom is doubled. To keep this course level, put a shingle at each corner of the building with the butt 1 inch below the sheathing. Tack a small nail to the bottom of each shingle and stretch a string between the two. Align all intervening shingles on the string line, being careful not to depress it.

For all successive courses tack a straight 1 by 4 across the shingles in line with the story pole marks and align the shingle butts on it.

If you are shingling an older house that is not level, the first course should follow the slant of the house rather than being level; otherwise, it will emphasize the irregularity. Adjust each successive course by ⅛ inch until the courses are level. This slight change will not be noticeable.

If you can't put the guide board between some windows, snap chalk lines between the story pole marks.

Fasten shingles with ring-shank galvanized nails to keep them from working loose. This is particularly important when nailing shingles to ⅜-inch plywood siding. Each shingle is nailed up with only two nails, regardless of its width. Place the nails 1 inch above the butt line for the next course and ¾ inch in from the edges.

Shingles can be spaced about ⅛ inch apart to allow for expansion. However, many shingles are being sold green, or freshly cut, and will shrink as they dry, so check with your dealer. No gap between shingles should be closer than 1½ inches to a gap in the course below, and no gap should be in line with one less than three courses below. When putting a course above a door or window, don't let a gap line up with the window or door edge.

Where shingles must be cut to fit around obstructions, measure and cut with a handsaw or a coping saw. For fine trimming when fitting along casing or trim boards, use a block plane on the shingle edge.

If shingles must be shortened to fit above a window or door opening, trim the shingles from the butt end. Trimming along the top will mean thicker shingles under the row above, causing a bulge.

Corner Treatments

Where shingles meet at corners, they can be mitered, woven, or butted against trim.

Mitering is the most painstaking method. Each shingle must be fitted against another, and the edges miter-cut with a power saw. Although mitered corners are very good-looking, they are the least effective at blocking wind-driven rain.

Woven corners provide better weather protection and are more commonly used, but they too must be individually fitted and then cut.

To weave corners nail the bottom layer of the doubled starter course around the bottom of the house. Now start the next layer of shingles. Consult the illustration to see how the top shingle on side A extends beyond the corner. Put the side B shingle against the extended shingle and trace its outline along the back of the side A shingle. Cut along that line with a keyhole saw, and nail the shingles in place.

On the next row up, repeat the process, this time extending the end shingle on side B beyond the corner and, on its back, marking the outline of the shingle on side A. Continue up the wall in this manner, with courses overlapping in alternate rows.

When you reach the final, or soffit, course, you may have to trim the tops of the shingles to make a good fit. After installing this course, crown the course by installing a molding to cover the crack at the soffit.

The most effective weather protection—and the fastest way to shingle corners—is to use corner trim boards. These should be at least 1 by 3 or 1 by 4 stock, but for a more pronounced effect use 2 by 3s or 2 by 4s. You can use redwood or cedar to weather naturally with the shingles, or paint the corner boards for contrast.

Place the boards on the corners with the edges overlapping to form a tight seal, then bring each course of shingles flush with the board edges. Use a plane to trim shingle edges where necessary for a smooth fit against the board.

Inside corners can also be woven, or shingle edges can be butted against a 2 by 2 set into the corner (see illustration).

Put a bead of caulk between the shingles and corner boards.

Wood Shingle Application

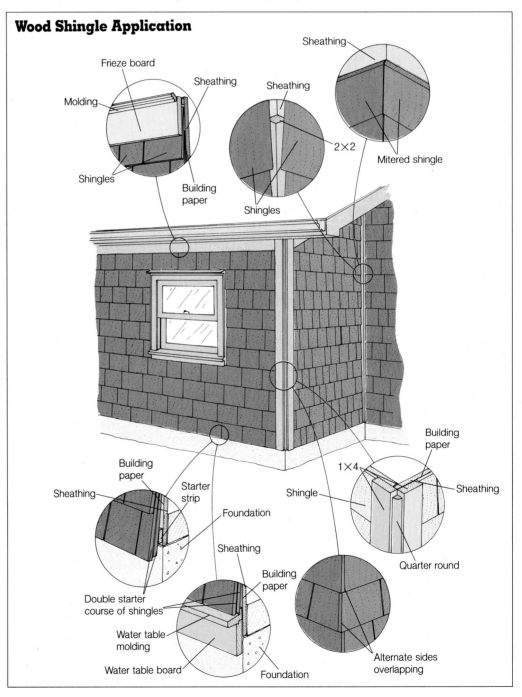

92

APPLYING STUCCO

Stucco is one of the more widely used sidings in this country because of its durable, weather-tight shield and low maintenance. But it has some drawbacks. It is hard to apply, and it may crack if poorly applied or if the house settles. Stucco can be applied by the careful do-it-yourselfer, but consider finding a pro to work with you or at least get you started.

Some General Considerations

Stucco is a mix of cement, sand, lime (to keep it plastic), and water. You can buy premixed sacks of the dry ingredients or mix your own. Stucco is applied in three separate coats over metal lath or chicken wire nailed to the sheathing. Special nails with fiber washers, called furring nails, are used to space the wire away from the building paper. The first coat, called the scratch coat, is about ¼ inch thick. It is supported on the wall by the metal lath or wire. Before the first coat dries, it is scored with a rakelike trowel called a scarifier so that the second coat will adhere to it. The second coat, called the brown coat because years ago it contained brown sand, is then troweled on about ⅜ to ½ inch thick. This coat must be put on smoothly and evenly, because the final finish coat, which is no more than ¼ inch thick, will not hide any mistakes.

The orientation of your house to the sun is an important consideration in applying stucco. If a wall has long exposure to hot afternoon sun, the stucco may dry too rapidly, shrink, and crack. This is particularly true with the thick second coat. If you have such a wall, plan your stuccoing for times of the day when direct sun will be minimal, or hang shade cloths from the eaves.

The best temperature range for applying stucco is between 50° and 80° F; it should not be applied when temperatures drop below 40° F, because it becomes too stiff to be applied properly.

Preparing the Wall

Stucco requires considerable preparation, and working with the reinforcing wire and metal lath sheets can be hard on hands and tempers. Be sure that you are committed to this project before beginning.

In New Construction

Cover the walls of the house with the cheapest exterior-grade ⅜-inch or ½-inch plywood. Cover this with building paper (similar to 15-pound felt) in horizontal strips overlapping 2 inches top to bottom and 4 inches end to end.

Now snap a level chalk line around the foundation about 6 inches from the ground. Along this line nail the reinforcing wire, called stop bead or weep screed, mesh side up. Use case-hardened masonry nails spaced every 8 inches.

Nail the stop bead around window and door casings every 6 inches, cutting it to length with tin snips. Keep the mesh pointing out. Now nail the stop bead around the top edge of the wall with the mesh pointing down in the same way.

Starting from the bottom at one corner and working up, nail on the metal lath sheets. Note that the nails are sold with the washers close to the nail head. Push the washers away from the nail head, hook the wire between the nail head and washers, then drive the nail home. Stretch the wire mesh each time you hook the nail. Note that the bottom of the first lath sheet rests in the stop bead.

Overlap the strips 1 inch where they meet horizontally and 2 inches at the ends. Place furring nails every 6 inches on the lath. Cut the sheets to fit into the stop bead around window and door openings.

At the corners nail a strip of corner bead vertically along the edge. The metal strip should protrude from the edge by ¾ inch. Use a level to make the bead vertical, and if more than one length must be used, carefully align the two ends. Double-check that the beads are accurately placed—they will be important guides when you apply the second coat.

With the metal lath all in place, the wall preparation is complete. Apply masking tape to door and window casings to protect them from stains.

Over Masonry Or Old Stucco

Stuccoing a masonry wall or stuccoing over old stucco does not require felt or the metal lath, nor is the first, or scratch, coat of stucco necessary.

First scrub the wall thoroughly with a wire brush to remove all dirt and loose or flaky material. Use a hose to spray the wall with water. After it dries, use a roller to coat the wall with a masonry bonding agent, available at hardware and paint stores. Let the bonding agent dry overnight, then go to the brown coat.

Mixing Stucco

Stucco must be mixed, just like the concrete that it is. The easiest way is to buy stucco mix and rent a stucco mixer big enough to handle one full sack. What you pay in rent will be more than made up for in saved time. Dump in the mix and add water until the mix is a soft, plastic consistency that you can squeeze and hold in your hand without any drips.

For small repair jobs, you can rent a stucco mixer or simply use a large metal mortar box, which you can either buy at your local hardware store or rent.

A standard mix is 3 parts building sand (as opposed to the finer mortar sand), 1 part portland cement, and ¼ part lime. The amount of water you must add will depend on how wet the sand is.

Put all the dry ingredients in the mortar box and turn the combination repeatedly with a flat-bottomed shovel until the mix is an even color. Push the

Stucco Application

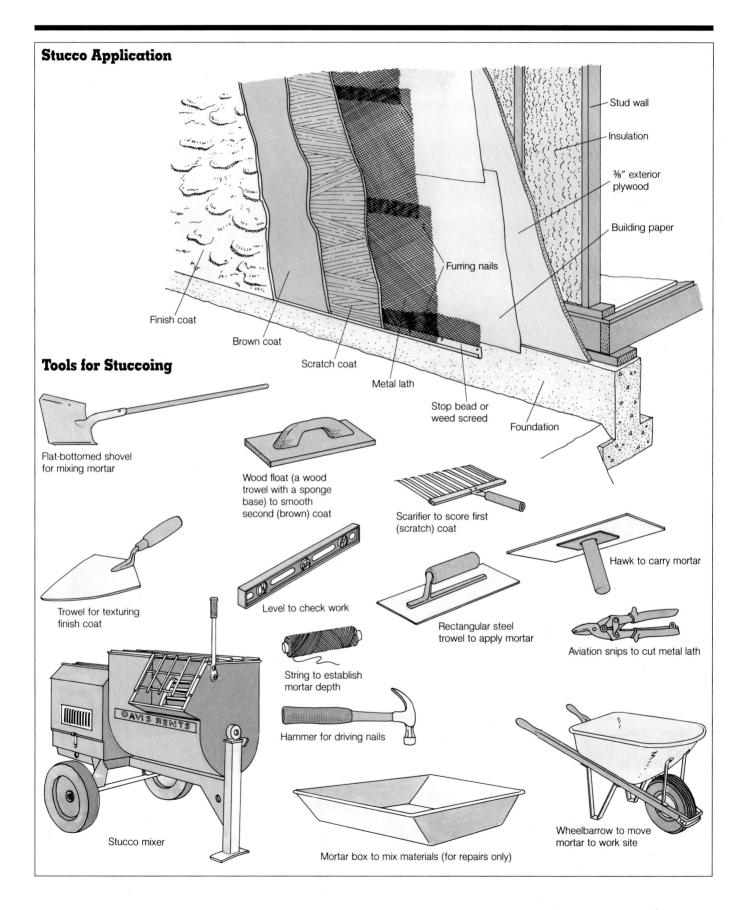

Stud wall

Insulation

⅜" exterior plywood

Building paper

Furring nails

Finish coat

Brown coat

Scratch coat

Metal lath

Stop bead or weed screed

Foundation

Tools for Stuccoing

Flat-bottomed shovel for mixing mortar

Wood float (a wood trowel with a sponge base) to smooth second (brown) coat

Scarifier to score first (scratch) coat

Hawk to carry mortar

Trowel for texturing finish coat

Level to check work

Rectangular steel trowel to apply mortar

Aviation snips to cut metal lath

String to establish mortar depth

Hammer for driving nails

DAVIS RENTS

Stucco mixer

Mortar box to mix materials (for repairs only)

Wheelbarrow to move mortar to work site

mix into half of the box. Slowly add water to the other side of the box while you keep mixing the dry ingredients into the water. When it looks almost right, be careful, because at this point you can make the mistake of adding too much water. The stucco should have a plastic consistency, neither dry nor soupy. If it is too soupy, add equal proportions of the dry ingredients until it is right.

One caution in new construction: Lumber is often sold green and will shrink as it dries. This can cause the stucco applied to it to crack. To prevent this, use lumber graded dry. Or you can apply the scratch coat to seal the house, then wait two to three months before applying the brown and finish coats.

Applying The Mortar

Once the mortar is mixed, take it to the work area in a wheelbarrow. It's now ready to be placed on a hawk and then troweled into the wall. If you are inexperienced and work slowly, keep the mortar covered with a piece of plastic to prevent its drying too fast. If it appears dry, stir it around but do not add more water.

You can place mortar directly on your hawk with a trowel, or keep a pile of it on a mortarboard made from a sheet of scrap plywood. Position the plywood over a couple of sawhorses near the wall.

Load the mortarboard, then chop the mortar with the edge of the trowel and spread it evenly around the center of the mortarboard. To load your trowel, cut through the mortar

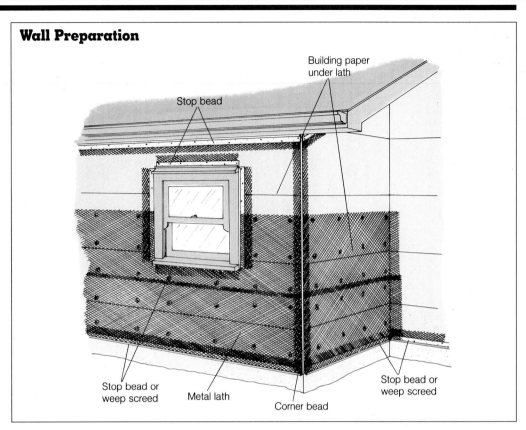

Wall Preparation

Building paper under lath

Stop bead

Stop bead or weep screed

Metal lath

Corner bead

Stop bead or weep screed

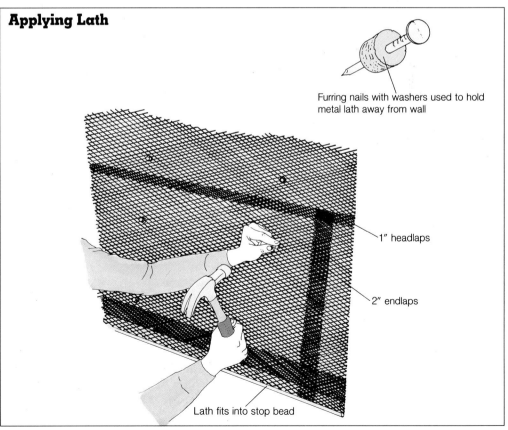

Applying Lath

Furring nails with washers used to hold metal lath away from wall

1" headlaps

2" endlaps

Lath fits into stop bead

Loading the Trowel

Scoop stucco onto upturned trowel

Mortar Application

Press mortar in with an even upward stroke

Scarifying the Scratch Coat

Make horizontal grooves with scarifier

on the side away from you, then simultaneously tilt the mortarboard down toward you while scooping the section of mortar off the board with the trowel, as shown. A few practice tries, while everyone watches you drop the mortar on the ground, will help you perfect this move. To keep the pile centered, turn the hawk a quarter-turn after each trowel load and take the mortar from the side away from you.

Apply the mortar at the top of the wall and work downward. As you press the mortar against the wall, tilt the top of the trowel slightly away from the wall and then apply the mortar with an upward sweep, pressing it into the metal lath.

Continue working your way downward, blending adjoining areas together with smooth, horizontal strokes.

Use this basic motion in applying each coat.

Scratch Coat

The first coat should be ¼ to ⅜ inch thick, with most of the mortar pressed behind the lath. Cover the lath evenly with just enough mortar for a faint

impression to show through. Check carefully to make sure that no bulges or pockets occur along the wall.

Before the mortar dries score it horizontally with the rake-like tines of the scarifier. The tines should bite deep enough to almost touch the lath without exposing it. The grooves created by the scarifier will make the next coat adhere.

When working on a long or high wall, make sure that the mortar doesn't dry before you scarify it. Allow the scratch coat to dry for four to six hours before proceeding.

Brown Coat

Before applying this coat—the most critical of the three because of the evenness required—two preparatory steps are necessary.

First, stretch strings horizontally across the wall. One string should be placed near the top of the wall, one near the bottom, and one (or more, if the wall is high) centered between the first two. Attach the strings to nails placed beyond the corners so that each string is held out from the wall

by the protruding stop beads. This space between the wall and string establishes the thickness of the brown coat. Every 5 feet along the string lines, drive a 3-inch galvanized roofing nail so that the head is just flush with the inside edge of the string. The nails will form vertical lines up the wall. Place nails about 12 inches away from both sides of doors and windows to form vertical lines. When the nails are all in, remove the strings.

The next step is to trowel on the screeds, which are narrow, vertical strips of stucco applied over the nails in a coat just thick enough to cover the nail heads. When the screeds are in place and have dried for 24 hours, the areas between them are filled in to the same thickness as the screeds, which serve as leveling guides.

Apply the stucco screeds from top to bottom, just covering the nail heads, in strips only as wide as the steel trowel. After each strip is applied, place a straight board on edge against the screed and smooth out any high or low spots before moving on to the next

screed. Let the screeds dry for 24 hours.

Before applying the brown coat, spray the wall lightly with water, with the hose nozzle set for misting. Dampen only as much wall as you think you can cover in an hour.

Apply the brown coat from top to bottom. Feather this coat into the screeds with smooth, even strokes so that no joints are visible. Smooth the mortar over the beads at the corners, top, and bottom.

Regularly check your work—sight down the wall and place a straightedge vertically along it. Use the straightedge in a sawing motion to shave off high points; fill in low spots with more mortar.

Allow each section between a pair of screeds to dry for an hour, then rub with a wood float in a circular motion. Rub lightly until you feel the sand in the brown coat just work to the surface. Let this coat dry for at least 24 hours, misting it gently every 4 hours to keep it from drying too rapidly. Protect it from sun with shade cloths or wet sheets draped on the wall to help hold in moisture.

Applying the Brown Coat

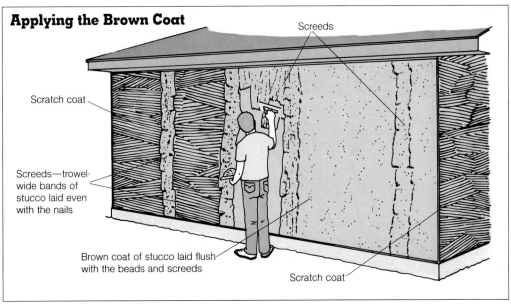

Screeds

Scratch coat

Screeds—trowel-wide bands of stucco laid even with the nails

Brown coat of stucco laid flush with the beads and screeds

Scratch coat

Finish Coat

The final coat, only ⅛ to ¼ inch thick, can be colored and textured according to your tastes. For various shades of brown, tan, or off-white, pigment available from your stucco supplier is mixed in the final coat. For a white finish, use white mortar and white sand.

The standard smooth-finish coat is troweled on just like the other coats and then, while still wet, is "floated" with a wood float. Go over the finish coat while it is still damp, working the float in a circular motion without leaving a pattern.

Many other patterns, as illustrated, can be obtained when applying the finish coat.

For the Modern American pattern, scrape the finish coat in vertical strokes with a 2 by 4 block just after surface moisture disappears. Press firmly enough to roughen the mortar without tearing it.

Applying the Finish Coat

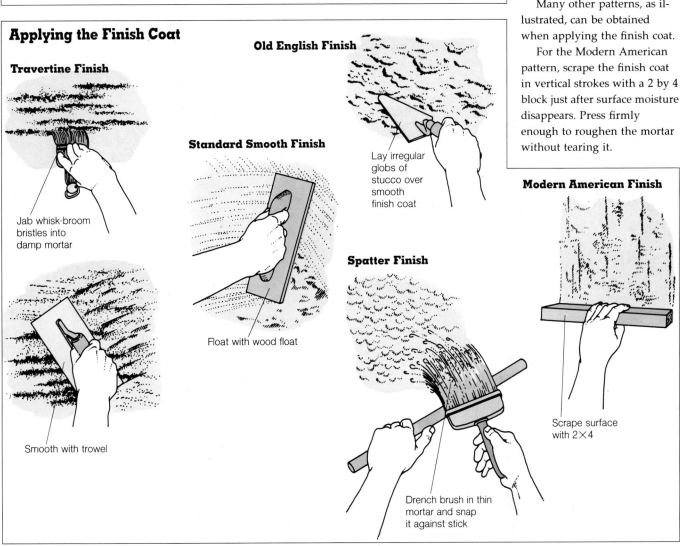

Travertine Finish

Jab whisk-broom bristles into damp mortar

Smooth with trowel

Old English Finish

Lay irregular globs of stucco over smooth finish coat

Standard Smooth Finish

Float with wood float

Spatter Finish

Drench brush in thin mortar and snap it against stick

Modern American Finish

Scrape surface with 2×4

For the travertine pattern, jab the bristles of a whisk broom into the mortar while it is still damp, working horizontally across the wall. Then go back over the mortar with a steel trowel in long, horizontal strokes to smooth the rough top edges of the mortar.

The spatter finish, commonly seen on houses more than 30 years old, is created by dipping a large brush in mortar mixed thinner than normal then snapping the brush against a stick to spatter the wall. Spray the wall in this fashion as evenly as possible. Let it dry for about an hour, then go back over it again until an even stippled effect is obtained.

For the rough effect of Old English stucco, first lay on a smooth, thin layer of finish coat. After it has dried for about an hour, use a round-nosed trowel to apply irregular gobs of mortar, as shown.

Stucco is widely used on Tudor, contemporary, and Spanish-style homes. It is difficult to apply, but once finished, requires little maintenance and can be simply washed down periodically to stay attractive.

STUCCO STONE AND BRICK

You can simulate the appearance of natural stone or brick siding with a variety of masonry veneers manufactured by several companies. Individually installed pieces are permanently attached to the exterior wall surface with mortar. Properly installed, masonry veneer is indistinguishable from the real thing.

In addition to the numerous patterns available, masonry veneers offer several advantages to the homeowner who wants the appearance of stone or brick but finds it financially out of reach. Material costs are much lower than stone or brick, and so are installation costs. Because of its light weight and quick adhesion characteristics to any wall in good condition, no structural changes, footings, or wall ties are required.

Masonry veneer can be applied directly to clean, untreated masonry, concrete, or stucco. If the surface has been painted or sealed or is dirty, it should be sandblasted clean before application. Building paper and an expanded metal lath are required on metal or wood surfaces.

Virtually all forms of masonry veneer are applied with mortar, although the exact application technique varies with the material being installed. For example, Cultured Brick® veneer and the surface to which it will be installed must be prewet with water so that the surface and back of the brick are damp during application. Mortar can be tinted to complement the color of the material being installed and to conceal joints between stones or bricks.

These noncombustible materials have an insulation value equivalent to approximately 14 inches of natural stone or 6 inches of common brick, and are maintenance-free. Because the color is an integral part of the casting process, it will not fade or otherwise lose its natural appearance.

Even an ordinary home can be transformed into a stone mansion with the use of a masonry veneer.

REPAIR & MAINTENANCE

No matter where you live, the roof and siding of your house are under year-round assault by wind, rain, heat, and possibly ice. Your best defense against this attack by the elements is a good maintenance program.

This chapter, by providing the details of caring for roofs, sidings, gutters, and downspouts, will help you spot problems before they develop into disasters. The information on fixing broken or bowed shingles, bubbles in tar and gravel roofs, and leaks in and around flashing will help you find and fix roof or siding problems before they become serious. Maintenance of gutters and downspouts is explained, and there are instructions on how to repair cracked, rotted, and damaged siding.

Autumn, before winter storms arrive, is a good time to tend to the maintenance of your home. Examine roofs and sidings, especially at joints and around flashings.

Your house is familiar to you, and because of that, you may not view it with a critical eye. So go on a walking tour with the idea of looking for trouble. Stand across the street and in the backyard for a good look at your roof. Use binoculars for a close look.

Pay special attention to the ridge, where roofing material generally comes loose first. If you can, go up on the roof and check the flashing around the vents and the chimney. Look for cracks in the shingles around the vents, or for dried and cracked roofing cement around vent flashing. If you have a chimney, see that the mortar holding the flashing is still sound, not loose and crumbling.

Shingles

All types of shingles can be repaired with minimal fuss.

Because shingles are small, self-contained units, they allow just the problem area to be tackled, without impacting the remainder of the roof.

Composition Shingles

If a shingle is torn or has only minor cracks, smooth roofing cement into the damaged area. Gently raise the butt of the shingle above the damaged spot and spread some cement underneath as a further precaution.

If a shingle has curled, put a coating of roofing cement under it and press it firmly back into place. Do the same for a shingle that has been blown out of position, and hold it in place with two roofing nails. Cover the nail heads with spots of roofing cement.

Missing and severely torn shingles must be replaced. A damaged shingle must be removed. In warm weather, which makes the shingles pliable, slide the straight end of a crowbar under the shingle to be removed and pry up the nails. This method has a hazard: It will lift the good shingle above the damaged one; in cool weather, the good shingle may break. A safer way is to slip a hacksaw blade under the shingle to be removed, cut each nail, and pull the shingle out.

To replace the shingle, carefully raise the one above, slide the new one in place, and nail. Put roofing cement under the edges of the new shingle and the one above to seal the repaired area.

Never attempt to replace just one tab of a torn shingle; always replace the entire shingle. However, you can make an effective (although less attractive) patch by slipping a piece of metal under the damaged shingle. Aluminum flashing, available in rolls at hardware stores, works well here. Cover the problem area with roofing cement, slip the metal in place, and nail it under the damaged shingle. Cover the nail heads with roofing cement as an extra precaution. The patch will not be particularly noticeable from the ground.

Wood Shakes And Shingles

Spaces between shakes and shingles are necessary to permit them to expand when wet,

Repairing a Cracked Shingle

Smooth roofing cement into crack

Replacing a Damaged Shingle

Pry out nails

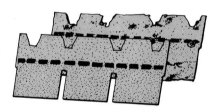

Notch the new shingle to match the tears made by nails in the old one

Fixing a Curled Shingle

Press shingle into roofing cement

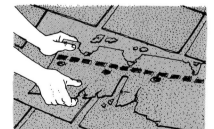

Pull out the damaged shingle

Nail new shingle into place

but a split shingle may let water through the roof. Small cracks in wood shingles or shakes can be filled with roofing cement. For a crack more than ½ inch wide, slide a piece of aluminum flashing material under the shingle. Put one nail on each side of the crack to hold the flashing, then coat the nail heads and flashing with roofing cement.

A fairly common problem with wood shingles and shakes is bowing. Since rain can blow into such gaps, they should be repaired. To fix a bowed shake or shingle, split it with a wood chisel. Remove a ⅛- to ¼-inch sliver along the split. Now nail the shingle down with one nail on each side of the split. Cover the split and the nail heads with roofing cement.

If a wood shingle or shake is badly cracked or rotted, it must be removed. First split it with a chisel and pull out the pieces. With a hacksaw blade cut the nails that held the old shingle. Trim a new shingle or shake to size and tap it into place, leaving it about ¾ inch lower than the butt line and remembering to allow ⅛- to ¼-inch clearance on each side. Nail it with two nails, angling them so that when the shingle or shake is driven into place, the nail heads are covered. Cover the nail heads with roofing cement.

Tar and Gravel

Flat roofs, or built-up roofs, are made of layers of heavy underlayment and tar with a fine gravel sprinkled on the final layer of tar to keep the sun from melting it. Leaks in these roofs are sometimes difficult to spot. A bubble in the roofing material is always suspect.

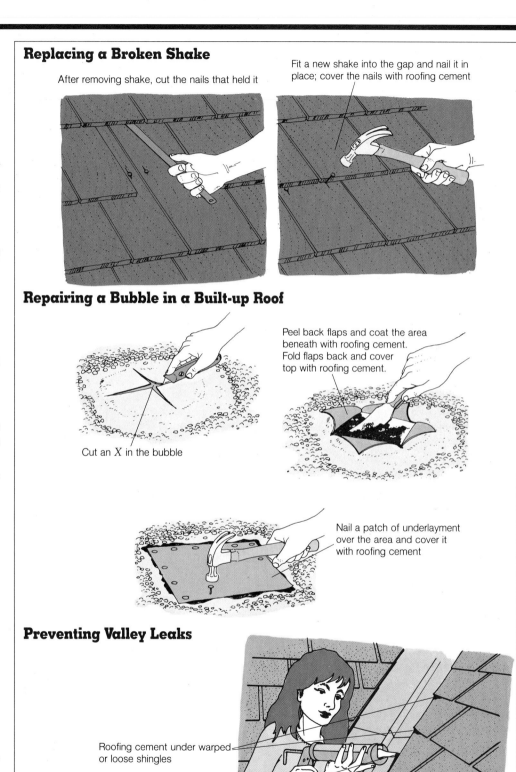

Replacing a Broken Shake

After removing shake, cut the nails that held it

Fit a new shake into the gap and nail it in place; cover the nails with roofing cement

Repairing a Bubble in a Built-up Roof

Cut an *X* in the bubble

Peel back flaps and coat the area beneath with roofing cement. Fold flaps back and cover top with roofing cement.

Nail a patch of underlayment over the area and cover it with roofing cement

Preventing Valley Leaks

Roofing cement under warped or loose shingles

Bead of roofing cement down the valley next to the shingles

However, don't repair bubbles unless they are visibly broken, or they may be the source of a leak in a low spot.

When repairing a bubble, first scrape away all the gravel around the area to be repaired. Next cut an *X* in the center of the bubble. Peel back each flap and liberally coat the area with roofing cement. Push the flaps back into place and cover the *X* and an 8-inch square around it with roofing cement. From roll roofing or 90-pound felt, cut a square patch 6 inches larger in each direction than the *X*. Nail the patch down with nails spaced 1 inch apart. Cover the patch and 2 inches beyond it with roofing cement.

Two key leak areas on built-up roofs are roof edges and flashing. If either seems suspicious, coat it liberally with roofing cement.

If the roof still leaks, it may be too old, and a new layer may be needed. Built-up roofs cannot be counted on to last much beyond 10 years. If you decide to have another layer put on, get a professional crew to do it. This is dangerous work—the tar pot can explode—and should not be attempted by the amateur. Get several estimates and ask for references. However, you might consider removing the old roof yourself (see page 30) and putting on a different sort of roof. It would probably cost about the same and be a more durable roof.

Tile

Remove any broken tile and install a new one in its place. Refer to pages 57 to 59 for instructions on installing tile.

Preventing Leaks Around Vent Pipes

Clean away debris and trim any badly cut shingles

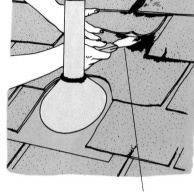

Roofing cement beneath any cracked or loose shingles near the vent

Metal and Vinyl Panels

If a panel is damaged, you'll need to replace the whole panel. See page 60 for instructions on installing panels.

Roll Roofing

Repair this type of roof as you would a tar and gravel one.

Flashing

If there is no obvious damage to your roof, such as missing shingles or shakes, leaks can probably to traced to one of the areas of flashing. See the first chapter for ways to locate leaks.

Valleys

Leaks in valleys are sometimes the result of a break in the metal flashing itself, but that is not common. If you do see a break, coat it with roofing cement, then cover it with a piece of aluminum patching tape, available in rolls. Cut off a length to amply cover the hole, peel off the protective backing, and stick the tape in place. Its bond increases over the years.

A more common cause of leaks in valley flashing is too much water for the valley. The water overflows the edges of the flashing and runs under the roofing material. To counter this, clear the valley of debris, which can act like a dam to back up water.

Next, make sure that the roofing material in the valley is cut in a smooth, straight line. If part of the material, such as a shingle, is sticking out into the valley, it can act as a diverter to turn water out of the valley and under the shingles.

To really ensure against valley leaks, carefully raise composition shingles where they meet the valley flashing and

coat the area with roofing cement. Then use a cartridge gun to run a bead of roofing cement down the valley flashing right next to the shingles. On the inflexible wood shingles, shakes, or tile, just run a bead of roofing cement along the edges where they extend onto the valley flashing.

Vents

Leaks often occur around vent pipes because the caulk or roofing cement has dried and shrunk or cracked. If this is the case, apply a new bead of roofing cement.

Check that the roofing surface around and above the vent pipe is in good condition. A crack in a shingle or tile will allow water to work its way under the metal flashing and down the vent pipe. It's a good practice to slightly raise the roofing material above the vent

Repairing Leaky Chimney Flashing

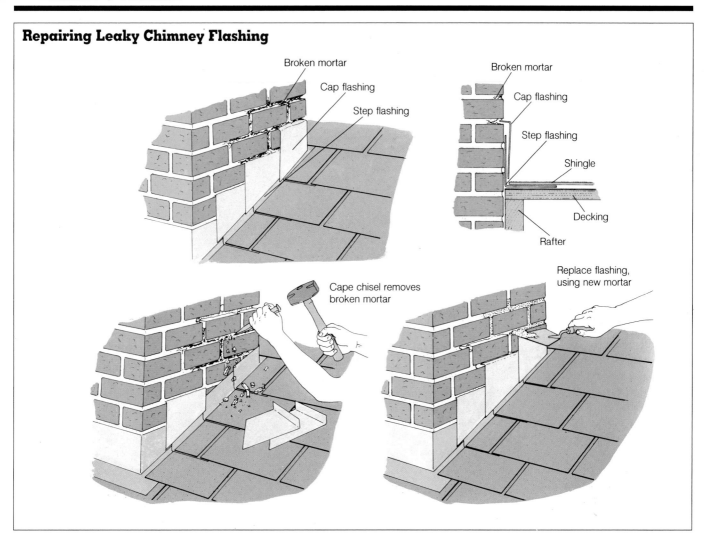

Broken mortar
Cap flashing
Step flashing

Broken mortar
Cap flashing
Step flashing
Shingle
Decking
Rafter

Cape chisel removes broken mortar

Replace flashing, using new mortar

flashing and caulk underneath with roofing cement.

One final item to check is that the roofing material around the flashing is cut smoothly. If part of a composition shingle, wood shingle, or shake protrudes slightly, it may divert water under the shingle. If you see such poor workmanship, trim with shears (a knife might cut the flashing metal) and seal with roofing cement.

On tile roofs, check that the concrete grout (mortar) around vents has not cracked. It can be sealed temporarily with roofing cement, but it should eventually be chiseled out and replaced with new grout.

Chimneys

Flashing around a chimney is made of aluminum, copper, or galvanized tin. Good flashing is in two stages, base and cap (see illustration). Most frequently, leaks originate where the cap flashing is set into mortar between the bricks. If there appears to be only a spot or two of loose mortar, scrape out the old material and fill the hole with butyl rubber caulk, which adheres well to masonry.

If the mortar is in poor condition, break it all out with a ⅜-inch cape chisel (a narrow-tipped cold chisel) and remove

the cap flashing. Remove old mortar to a depth of at least ½ inch, then clean the area thoroughly with a wire brush.

Old and new mortar do not bond well to each other. One solution is to coat old mortar with a bonding agent, available at hardware stores. Another is to soak old mortar and surrounding bricks with water. This helps prevent their drawing too much moisture out of the new mortar, weakening it.

For the patching material, use a premixed mortar or make your own from 1 part mortar cement and 3 parts fine sand. When the flashing has been reinstalled, give yourself some

added protection by coating the seams with butyl rubber caulk.

Heating Coils

If you live in an area with heavy snowfall, roof maintenance might include installing heating coils along the eaves. The coils, available at hardware stores and roofing companies, are clipped to shingles in a zigzag pattern along the eaves and plugged into an outside outlet. The heat prevents formation of ice dams along the eaves. Ice dams can cause water to back up under the shingles and into the house.

CARING FOR GUTTERS AND DOWNSPOUTS

From a ladder inspect your gutters. Look for breaks in the gutters and broken support straps. Poke the wood at the eaves under the shingles with a screwdriver to see if it's still firm. Soft wood, which almost resembles paper pulp, is a sign of rot.

Their Importance

An important aspect of house maintenance is a good gutter and downspout system that carries water away from the house. Without such a system, water will erode the ground beneath the eaves and is likely to run into the crawl space or basement of your house, where it will encourage wood rot and termites. In addition, a gutter system in poor repair allows water and ice to back up under shingles along the eaves, which can cause leaks in the house and wood rot on the roof.

If your house does not have a gutter and downspout system, it should. New installation is covered on pages 42 to 43. If your house does have such a system, it should be kept in good repair.

Regular Inspections

You might be surprised how much a twice-annual inspection of your gutters will prolong their life. Each spring and fall, clean the gutters and leaf traps of all debris. Put a hose into the downspout and make sure that the water runs freely.

If there appears to be a blockage in the downspout, full water pressure from the hose may clear it. If not, run a plumber's snake, the kind used for cleaning clogged sewer lines, into the downspout.

After cleaning, stand back and visually inspect the gutters and downspouts. Check that leaf traps are in place. If you live in a freezing climate, make sure that the ice did not misalign the drain system. Check that all the joints are still tight and there are no sags. Standing water in a gutter indicates sagging at that spot. Gutters should drop 1 inch for every 20 feet of run. Look carefully for loose nails or hanger straps on both the gutters and the downspouts.

Common Repairs

After cleaning the gutters, hose them out and inspect for damage. Here are some common problems and their solutions.

Sagging Gutters

A sagging gutter often indicates a broken support. Prop the gutter into place by wedging a long 2 by 4 under it. Look at the type of gutter hanger you have and compare it to those illustrated on page 43.
• If the strap has separated from the hanger, drill a hole through the strap and hanger and join them with a nut and bolt.
• If the rivet holding the hanger to the gutter is broken, drill out the rivet and replace it with a galvanized nut and bolt.

• If the strap extending under the roofing material is broken, cut it in half and remove the piece that extended under the roof. Replace it with a spike-and-ferrule hanger.

Holes in Gutters

No matter what gutters are made of, they will eventually develop holes through rust, rot, or punctures.

To repair holes in metal or vinyl gutters, first clean the area thoroughly with steel wool, working on the inside of the gutter. Small holes, the size of a nail, can be fixed with epoxy resin, available in most hardware stores.

Cover larger holes with an adhesive-backed aluminum tape which is then covered by a layer of roofing cement.

Wood gutters can develop holes through wood rot. To repair these you must wait until the wood is thoroughly dry. Poke suspected areas with a screwdriver and watch for the soft, flaky wood that indicates wood rot.

Chisel out all the bad wood and then soak the hole with pentachlorophenol wood preservative. When it is dry, fill the hole with plastic wood and smooth carefully until it conforms to the gutter outline. Give the repair a protective coat of roofing cement.

Leaking Joints

The final common problem with gutters is the joints. They separate because of loose hangers, ice loads, the weight of soggy leaves, and just old age. If you find a leaking joint, check for any loose hangers nearby and fix that problem first. On aluminum and galvanized steel gutters, use a caulking gun to squeeze silicone or butyl rubber caulk into the joint. With wood gutters, wait until the wood is completely dry and then apply butyl rubber caulk.

These metal gutters have a classic ogee design. The downspout curves are assembled from ready-made pieces. The downspout is placed near the corner trim to make it less prominent.

Look carefully at your siding material, with an eye out for loose, split, or rotting boards or shingles. Make a list of all the potential trouble spots you've seen on your tour, then read on for the solutions.

Board Siding

There may be problems with splitting in board siding, especially in areas of extreme weather. But split boards are easily repaired or replaced.

Repairing Split Boards

A siding board may split near an end where it was nailed. This should be repaired immediately to prevent rainwater from leaking into the stud cavity. Don't pull the nail where the wood split; you will mar the siding in the process. Use a chisel to pry the split farther apart, then coat the interior of the split with an epoxy resin glue, which is waterproof.

When the glue is tacky, push the split together again.

To prevent further splitting, use a push drill with a bit half the size of an 8-penny (8d) casing nail to drill holes on both sides of the split over the stud: nail. If there is no stud to nail to, try to drive shingle shims on both sides of the split to hold it until the glue dries. Set the nails; cover with wood putty that matches the house paint.

If you used a white glue, sand the glue surface lightly when it is dry and then repaint it, or the glue will not last through the winter.

Replacing Boards

If a siding board is badly splintered or rotted, it must be replaced.

Tongue-and-Groove

To remove and replace a section of tongue-and-groove boards, first locate the nearest studs on each side of the damaged area. This may be difficult, since tongue-and-groove siding is blind-nailed—that is, you can't see any exposed nail heads. One way is to use a stud finder, an inexpensive magnetic device that finds nails in studs. You can also measure from one corner of the house, keeping in mind that studs are generally placed every 16 inches on center. Tap the boards until you hear a solid rather than a hollow sound.

Cuts in the board section to be removed must be made

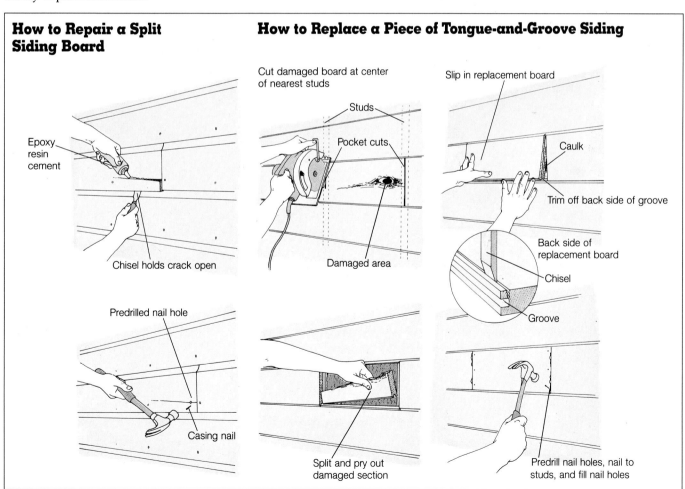

How to Repair a Split Siding Board

Epoxy resin cement

Chisel holds crack open

Predrilled nail hole

Casing nail

How to Replace a Piece of Tongue-and-Groove Siding

Cut damaged board at center of nearest studs

Studs

Pocket cuts

Damaged area

Split and pry out damaged section

Slip in replacement board

Caulk

Trim off back side of groove

Back side of replacement board

Chisel

Groove

Predrill nail holes, nail to studs, and fill nail holes

How to Replace a Piece of Lapped Siding

Patching a Crack in Stucco

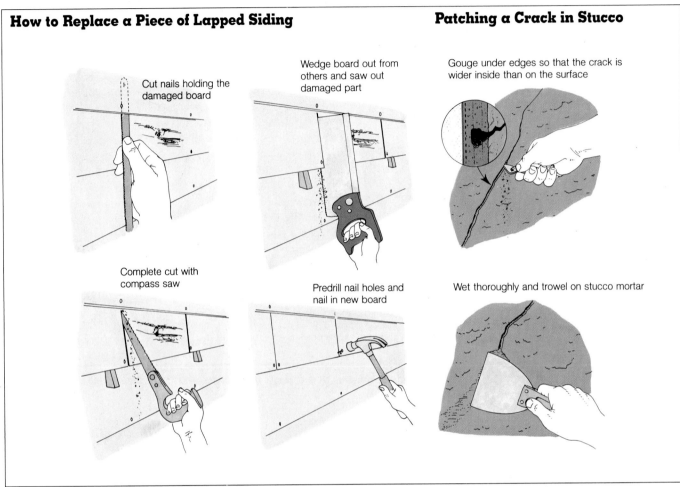

Cut nails holding the damaged board

Wedge board out from others and saw out damaged part

Gouge under edges so that the crack is wider inside than on the surface

Complete cut with compass saw

Predrill nail holes and nail in new board

Wet thoroughly and trowel on stucco mortar

down the center of a stud so that there will be backing for the new piece. Mark the line, then use a circular saw to make a pocket cut on the line. Do this by raising the blade guard, resting the saw on the front of the baseplate, starting the saw, and gently lowering the blade into the board. Do not cut the adjacent boards; instead, finish the cuts with a chisel. Now split the section down the middle with the chisel, or cut it with the saw, and pry out. Remove any nails.

To slip the replacement board in place, first trim off the back side of the groove, as illustrated, then slip the board in place and nail it to the studs.

Set the nail heads and cover with wood putty.

Lapped

Siding such as clapboard, shiplap, and other styles of lapped siding is removed in much the same way as is tongue-and-groove. Cuts should be centered down the studs nearest each side of the damaged area. Lapped siding is somewhat easier to remove, because it is not locked in with a tongue-and-groove system. Use a chisel to pry out the center part of the board, then slip wedges of wood shingle under the siding near both ends to hold it out. Cut the boards with a circular saw as described above or with

a backsaw. Finish the cut with a keyhole saw. Caulk the edges of the new piece, then fit in place and nail.

Plywood Siding

Because of plywood's inherent strength, damage is not common. Should your siding be damaged, however, it is usually best to replace the entire panel, since a patched section will be quite noticeable. To replace a panel, remove any battens over the edges, pull the nails along the edges, and take off the panel. Nail the replacement in place, then paint or stain to match the rest of the siding.

Shake and Wood Shingle Siding

Repair damaged shake or wood shingle siding as you would a roof (see pages 102 to 103).

Stucco Siding

Cracks are the most common problem in stucco siding. To fix them use the point of a can opener to gouge out the stucco under each edge of the crack in a bell shape. This provides a key for the repair material to lock into. Buy a small package of premixed stucco mortar and mix with water until it is a thick, creamy texture. Thoroughly wet the crack, then trowel mortar into it and smooth over. The mortar comes in colors, but you will probably have to paint the affected side of the house for a finished appearance.

Vinyl Or Metal Siding

Damaged vinyl or metal siding is repaired by replacing the panel. Dents in aluminum siding can often be removed without panel replacement; scratches sometimes can be minimized with the use of touch-up paint.

Replacing A Vinyl Panel

You'll need an unlocking device (also called a zip tool) to remove the damaged panel. This simple device has an end shaped to match the panel locking strip. The end of the tool is hooked into the locking strip of the panel above the damaged one. By applying a firm, downward pressure on the tool and sliding it the length of the panel, you can free the panel enough to reach underneath and lift it up. Prop up the panel with one or two small blocks of wood and remove the nails holding the damaged panel in place. After locking and nailing the replacement panel in position, use the unlocking tool to relock the upper panel in place.

Replacing An Aluminum Panel

Carefully cut a slit along the center of the damaged panel with a utility knife; if the panel simulates a double row of siding,

make the cut just above the center of the damaged panel. After cutting, disengage and remove the lower section of the damaged panel.

Trim the nailing and locking strip from the replacement panel, then run a healthy bead of roofing cement along the entire length of the damaged half of the panel remaining on the wall.

To install the replacement panel, slip its upper edge beneath the locking hook of the panel above the damaged area, then lock it into the lip of the panel below. Apply firm pressure over the area of the cement bead so that it will adhere to the replacement panel.

Removing A Dent From an Aluminum Panel

Panel replacement is probably the best answer when you have numerous small dents, such as those resulting from a heavy hailstorm. The following procedure works best on a circular dent, such as that resulting from a ball striking the panel; it is not as useful when the damage takes the form of a crease.

Fit a rubber grommet or several washers on the end of a small sheet-metal screw and thread the screw into the center of the dent. Using a pair of pliers, grasp the head of the screw and pull outward on the screw until the dent has popped or flattened out. Depending upon the particular dent, this technique will work either perfectly or almost perfectly.

Remove the screw from the panel and fill the hole with plastic aluminum, available in hardware stores. Apply it as neatly as possible, then let the

material harden. By careful filing, sanding, and touching up with matching paint, you can eliminate the hole and restore the panel's appearance.

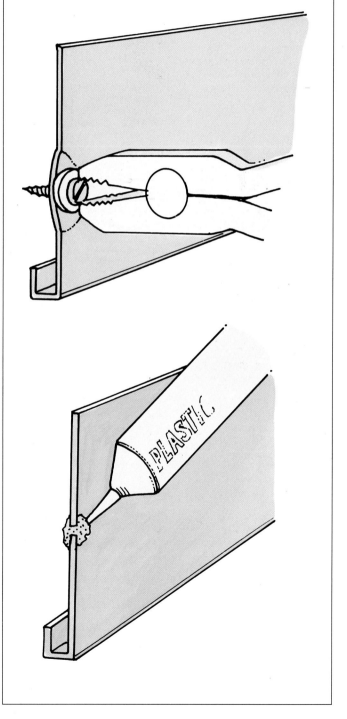

Pulling a Dent From an Aluminum Panel and Filling With Plastic Aluminum Adhesive

INDEX

U.S./Metric Measure Conversion Chart

	Symbol	When you know:	Multiply by:	To find:			
		Formulas for Exact Measures			**Rounded Measures for Quick Reference**		
Mass (Weight)	oz	ounces	28.35	grams	1 oz		= 30 g
	lb	pounds	0.45	kilograms	4 oz		= 115 g
	g	grams	0.035	ounces	8 oz		= 225 g
	kg	kilograms	2.2	pounds	16 oz	= 1 lb	= 450 g
					32 oz	= 2 lb	= 900 g
					36 oz	= 2¼ lb	= 1000 g (1 kg)
Volume	tsp	teaspoons	5.0	milliliters	¼ tsp	= $\frac{1}{24}$ oz	= 1 ml
	tbsp	tablespoons	15.0	milliliters	½ tsp	= $\frac{1}{12}$ oz	= 2 ml
	fl oz	fluid ounces	29.57	milliliters	1 tsp	= $\frac{1}{6}$ oz	= 5 ml
	c	cups	0.24	liters	1 tbsp	= ½ oz	= 15 ml
	pt	pints	0.47	liters	1 c	= 8 oz	= 250 ml
	qt	quarts	0.95	liters	2 c (1 pt)	= 16 oz	= 500 ml
	gal	gallons	3.785	liters	4 c (1 qt)	= 32 oz	= 1 liter
	ml	milliliters	0.034	fluid ounces	4 qt (1 gal)	= 128 oz	= 3¾ liter
Length	in.	inches	2.54	centimeters	⅜ in.	= 1 cm	
	ft	feet	30.48	centimeters	1 in.	= 2.5 cm	
	yd	yards	0.9144	meters	2 in.	= 5 cm	
	mi	miles	1.609	kilometers	2½ in.	= 6.5 cm	
	km	kilometers	0.621	miles	12 in. (1 ft)	= 30 cm	
	m	meters	1.094	yards	1 yd	= 90 cm	
	cm	centimeters	0.39	inches	100 ft	= 30 m	
					1 mi	= 1.6 km	
Temperature	° F	Fahrenheit	⅝ (after subtracting 32)	Celsius	32° F	= 0° C	
	° C	Celsius	⅝ (then add 32)	Fahrenheit	68°F	= 20°C	
					212° F	= 100° C	
Area	in.²	square inches	6.452	square centimeters	1 in.²	= 6.5 cm²	
	ft²	square feet	929.0	square centimeters	1 ft²	= 930 cm²	
	yd²	square yards	8361.0	square centimeters	1 yd²	= 8360 cm²	
	a.	acres	0.4047	hectares	1 a.	= 4050 m²	